Belongs To

Marcellus
Dosen't
Own
This

To

CHRIS

Scott

Books No
anymore else

SCUBA, SPEAR, AND SNORKEL

SCUBA SPEAR AND SNORKEL

by
Larry Bortstein
and
Henry Berkowitz

Illustrated by
Frank Bolle

Cowles Book Company, Inc.
New York

Acknowledgment:
We wish to thank Mr. Sam Davison of The Dacor Corporation of
Northfield, Ill., for his assistance in the preparation of this volume.
The illustrations of all gear and equipment in these
pages are photographs of Dacor products.

Contents

1. History of Diving   7

2. Physical Fitness for Diving   15

3. Skin and Scuba Diving Equipment   21

4. Basic Diving Techniques   47

5. Diving Safety and First Aid   65

6. Spearfishing   93

7. Underwater Photography   103

8. Catching and Maintaining
   Saltwater Fish   111

9. Dangerous Marine Life   115

10. Experiences of a Diver   129

Epilogue   137

Decompression Procedures   144

Glossary   151

Index   157

1.

History of Diving

AS MAN HAS SOUGHT new frontiers to conquer through the passing years, he naturally has focused his attention more and more upon the sea. Although his exploits in outer space have perhaps been more publicized, man has probed even further into the depths of the sea as he develops better explorative mechanisms and techniques. Indeed, research reveals that man has always been curious about the abundance to be found in the sea.

Even prehistoric man attempted free diving—diving without breathing apparatus. Records show that as early as 3,000 B.C., man attempted to penetrate the surface of the oceans for food, but was foiled by his physical limitations—that is, the inability to remain underwater for long periods without breathing. Sponge "farmers" in Crete were diving below the seas between 3,000 and 1,400 B.C. As far back as 900 B.C., Assyrians, breathing from air bladders which they carried underwater, made forays into the depths of the sea.

The First Diving Bell

Alexander the Great, one of the great leaders in ancient times, made a major contribution to diving history in 333 B.C. He encouraged the development of a diving bell, a concept that had been hinted at hundreds of years before, but carried to completion by the Macedonian ruler. His motives were not what one would consider wholesome; he wanted an underwater force to destroy the defenses of Tyre when he attacked that island city.

The diving bell represented a marked improvement in extending the time a diver might stay underwater, since it reduced the number of times the diver would be forced to surface for air. However, depth-pressure factors and the bell's limited air capacity still created problems that were not satisfactorily resolved for several centuries.

Nevertheless, there have been countless attempts at improvements over the years. In 77 A.D., Pliny the Elder described a breathing device similar to the snorkel used by modern skin divers. About 100 B.C., Swedish divers sank enemy ships by cutting holes in them under the water line. Spanish sailors of an early era placed buckets over their heads when they went underwater to seek treasure from ships that had been sunk.

The lust for treasure inspired another breakthrough in diving apparatus in 1538, in Toledo, Spain, a city celebrated in art by the Greek painter El Greco. Before the skeptical eyes of Emperor Charles V and members of his court, a pair of Grecian inventors unveiled a large inverted "kettle" from which burned a light. The inventors entered the kettle, which was open at the bottom, by placing it over their heads, had the kettle lowered into the water, and then raised. Amazingly, the clothing of the Greeks was found to be dry upon surfacing, and the light still burned brightly. This diving kettle preceded the more sophisticated diving casks of Captain William Phipps, an American seaman from Boston. Phipps inverted casks, weighted the open ends with lead, and lowered them 65 feet down on Silver Shoals. By obtaining breaths of air from these casks while underwater, divers were able to remain below for 20 minutes with Phipps' creation.

In 1880 Giovanni Borelli of Italy designed a self-contained, re-circulating air device that could be operated by the diver manipulating a piston pump by hand. Thirty-six years later, an Englishman, Dr. Edmund Halley, devised a method by which divers could stay submerged for periods of up to one and one-half hours. He sent barrels of fresh air down to divers, using diving bells made of wood and bound with metal strips. Like the devices of Captain Phipps, Dr. Halley's bells were open at the bottom and weighted.

By the end of the 18th century, the innovators in the underwater submersion field had recognized the necessity for a diving suit. A German named Kleingert unveiled such a suit in 1798, but it had serious limitations. Augustus Siebe, an Englishman, corrected many of these drawbacks with the suit he devised in 1819. He invented diving equipment consisting of a metal helmet that enclosed the head and rested upon the diver's shoulders, enabling the diver to receive air through a hose connected to an air-compressing pump on the surface. Although this mechanism restricted movement underwater, it produced submersion times that had never been previously attained with any other device.

Siebe progressed further in his development of diving equipment and in 1837 introduced a completely enclosed, successfully pressurized, insulated suit to be worn with the helmet he had devised eighteen years earlier. However, this suit still was regulated by a pump from the surface, although some thought already was being given to a "self-contained underwater breathing apparatus" or scuba.

Meanwhile, in the late nineteenth century, a pair of Frenchmen, Rouquayrol and Denayrouse, made a contribution to diving equipment when they replaced the air hose with a tank of compressed air which could be carried on the diver's back. Breathing was handled through a regulator.

In many diving circles, scuba was originally considered impractical and not worth further consideration. Many skeptics believed that the small advantage gained in mobility with the use of scuba did not sufficiently make up for the loss in submersion time due to the limited capacity of scuba air containers.

However, as it had in the case of Alexander the Great centuries before, war created a need for advanced diving technology. With the advent of World War I, there came about a twofold need for scuba: as a submarine escape device, and as a protection against poisonous gases in the water. The United States government adopted a machine developed in 1902 by R. H. Davis for these purposes. The mechanism—a re-breathing scuba—filtered exhaled oxygen through purifying chemicals, making it possible to breathe the same oxygen over again.

A Weight Used for Descent

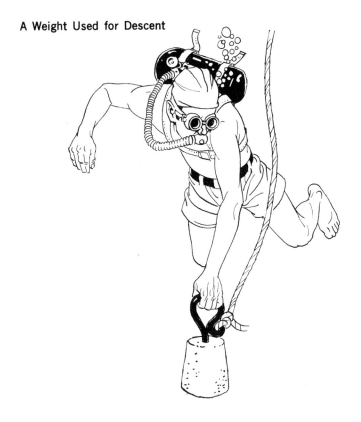

Another advance was made in 1925 when Commander Le Prieur of the French Navy introduced a scuba unit with a cast-iron tank that enabled the diver to breathe compressed air. This unit consisted of a mouthpiece and an intake hose attached to a regulator valve that controlled the flow of air emitted from the container to be inhaled. An exhaust valve in the mouthpiece allowed exhaled air to escape into the water. Though this apparatus proved very workmanlike, automation soon was to make it obsolete since a diver had to control the Le Prieur scuba by hand.

In 1934 the Tritonia Corporation of Glasgow, Scotland, manufactured a metal, self-contained diving apparatus for use in salvaging the *Lusitania,* a British ship that had been torpedoed and sunk by the Germans off the Southeastern tip of Ireland on May 7, 1915. Technically, the Tritonia mechanism was the most sophisticated diving apparatus created up to that time. In it the diver could breathe an oxygen mixture at atmospheric pressure, with no interference from the water pressure. In addition, he could be lowered and raised quickly with special equipment on the surface. However, the apparatus had one major drawback that made it nearly inoperable: it weighed 920 pounds!

To meet this serious deficiency, the Craig-Nohl self-contained helium-oxygen diving unit was launched in 1935. With this unit the diver could function in an atmosphere of helium and oxygen that was absorbed through a re-breather system. Furthermore, he could wear the old conventional diving suit. In 1937 Max Gene Nohl achieved a world record dive of 420 feet using this apparatus.

Not satisfied with their improvements, John Craig and Max Nohl, in conjunction with Dr. Edgar End of the Marquette University Medical School in Milwaukee and Jack Browne, produced in 1938 a "lung" that removed the heavy head equipment from the diver. With this gear, a diver could function under the

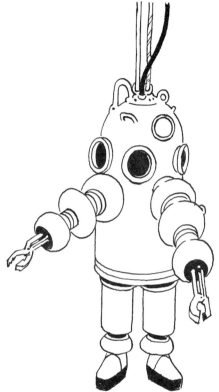

An Early Diving Suit

sea with almost limitless mobility.

World War II interrupted the development of the "lung" but Browne came up with his own designed oxygen lung, which was manufactured under the DESCO imprint, and subsequently used by U.S. Navy "frogmen" during the war. Browne also produced a diving mask, worn across the face with an air hose attached through which air was pumped from the surface. This hookah device further reduced the weight of the diver's equipment but, because of the connection of the hose to the surface, curtailed his underwater movements.

Taking full cognizance of the deficiencies in nearly all underwater diving mechanisms developed through the first four decades of this century, a pair of Frenchmen, Captain Jacques-Yves Cousteau and Emile Gagnan, set out in the early nineteen-forties to construct the ultimate in diving equipment—an apparatus that would afford the diver the best combination of mobility and long-lasting air supply. Finally, in 1943, came the revolution in diving technique that had been sought for so long.

It was the aqualung, a unit composed of a pressurized air tank, a mouthpiece, an intake hose, an exhaust hose, and an air-flow regulator valve that automatically allowed for the increases and decreases in the diver's demand for air. This is still the basic type of aqualung used today, though there have been further refinements made on the Cousteau-Gagnan device.

The aqualung had the effect of turning scuba diving from an almost exclusively utilitarian activity into one of the most pleasurable sports on earth. In nearly every section of the world thousands of people dive underwater annually in quest of fish, plant life, photographs—and just sheer fun.

Of course, the aqualung and similar equipment have also led to increased exploration of the sea, and to a growing number of individuals who have made exploration of the sea their life's work.

Scott Carpenter, one of America's pioneers in the exploration of space, left the company of the astronauts several years ago to become an aquanaut, where he could delve further into the great unknown expanse of the world's waters.

Whether you wish to become another Scott Carpenter or just want to experience the joys of scuba diving as a sport, this book will tell you how to go about making the most of your dreams. Read on and happy diving!

2.

Physical Fitness for Diving

ONE OF THE BEST FEATURES of scuba diving is that it is a sport in which almost any man, woman, or child can take part. However, this can be misleading, inasmuch as diving is a strenuous activity for which all would-be participants must be sufficiently prepared.

Even the most expert of divers never overextend themselves, and these individuals are better prepared for diving than the more casual participants in the sport. Therefore, it behooves anyone planning to undertake the activity to understand the physical requirements involved.

One point must be stressed above all others: *all would-be divers should have a complete physical examination before they make their first dive.* Most organizations concerned with underwater activities require thorough medical checkups by all prospective participants. Many of these organizations also attempt to ascertain whether candidates are in proper physical shape, either through special fitness tests or through checking their swimming ability. You do not have to belong to an organization to take part in diving, but you should have the same concern for the health and fitness standards these organizations demand.

Since diving is an activity that places great stress on the body, there can be no overemphasizing the need for physical fitness on the part of all divers. A diver with a serious defect is asking for trouble—not only for himself, but for anyone who may have to come to his assistance in the water.

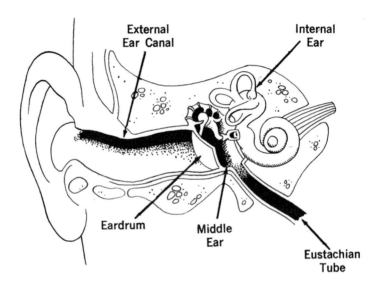

Sooner or later every diver is called upon to place stress on his strength and endurance. Even the best scuba equipment makes the work of breathing more difficult, and the extra effort involved in breathing adds a measure of exertion to the diver's activities while he is underwater. Lifting and carrying tanks and other equipment on dry land also represent hard work. Obviously, someone who has difficulty with these activities even before he goes into the water would be ill-advised to dive.

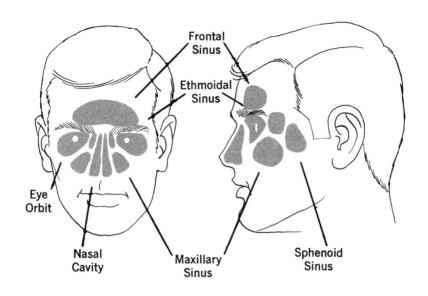

One absolute physical requirement for diving is the ability of the middle ear and sinuses to equalize pressure changes. A history of ear disorders usually dictates against diving, but much depends on the particular individual. A more serious case is made against an individual with a perforated tympanic membrane, since there would almost be no way for him to prevent water from entering the middle ear.

Particular attention should be paid, also, to a would-be diver's nose and throat history. A prospective diver should have no record of chronic tonsillitis, colds, and/or other throat infections and sinusitis. Needless to say, anyone with difficulties in either the respiratory or circulatory system should not expect to become a diver. Furthermore, a hypertense person possibly wouldn't be able to function in a calm and effective manner while underwater.

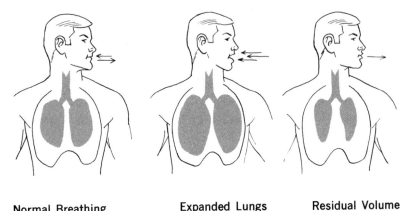

Normal Breathing   Expanded Lungs   Residual Volume

Other, less obvious areas where difficulty might occur if the
diver doesn't take proper precautions are the eyes and the teeth.
A diver's eyes should be able to correctly gauge light and distance. If he has an eye condition requiring him to wear spectacles, this does not necessarily rule out diving for him. He can
wear a mask with built-in prescription glasses to fit his needs, or
use a mask with a special device to keep his regular spectacles in
place.

A diver's teeth should be strong enough to enable him to effect
a solid, comfortable grip on the mouthpiece. Malocclusions or
other adverse mouth conditions should not be present, and any
individual who wears bridgework or false dentures should consult
a dentist before he attempts to dive.

Assuming your health allows you to take part in the thrilling
sport of diving, bear in mind that physical fitness must be strictly
maintained. For anyone with intentions of making diving a
regular activity, time out should be taken each day for a program of carefully planned physical activity.

The best conditioning exercise for a diver is swimming. Running also helps develop a part of the body used in diving. Swimming, however, conditions the diver in several ways, not the least of which is that it gives him the benefit of added time in the water.

Many divers claim they dive although they are not adept swimmers. While it is true that good swimming ability is not necessary for diving, there are obvious advantages for a diver who swims well. For one thing, anyone who has developed his swimming capacity is more likely to feel at home in the water and less likely to be subject to feelings of tension below the surface. For another, it is entirely possible that a diver may be faced with the accidental loss of his swim aids, and be compelled to resort to his own aquatic ability and judgment. Ideally, you should be able to swim two hundred yards without swim aids, swim fifty feet underwater without swim aids, and tread water for fifteen minutes before trying diving. Another valid test you can set for yourself would be to swim fifty yards with a leaden belt around the waist. This will enable you to simulate actual diving with ten pounds of scuba equipment.

As with all sports, diet plays an important role in diving. Fat is a serious threat to a diver, because excess weight affects his agility, coordination, and metabolism, in addition to making him more susceptible to the "bends." Generally speaking, a good diet for a diver would consist of high protein, low carbohydrate, and moderate fat foods during each meal.

If you have met your own—and a doctor's—standard of physical condition and fitness, and are ready to begin diving, you should avail yourself of a standard course in skin diving given by a certified instructor. Most local YMCAs across the country offer such courses, under the auspices of the National Association of Underwater Instructors.

In addition to receiving instruction in the uses of various

pieces of equipment, the diving student should learn (1) how to develop breath control when using the equipment; (2) how to enter and leave the water properly; (3) panic prevention exercises; (4) exercises to aid in body control; (5) how to adjust to changes of pressure.

The greatest change in pressure occurs between sea level and 33 feet. One cubic foot of air at sea level is reduced to one-half cubic foot 33 feet below sea level. Since most skin diving is done within 33 feet below the surface, the skin diver is subjected to this extreme pressure each time he enters and re-enters the water. To combat the effect of this pressure, the diver must practice swallowing, moving jaws from side to side, and blowing through nostrils into the faceplate while it is pressed against the nose.

Above all, before making your first dive, let your own common sense guide you. Don't let the fact that diving is a fun activity delude you into thinking you can prepare for it lightly. A wise man summed it up a long time ago when he said: look before you leap.

3.

Skin and Scuba Diving Equipment

DIVING IS LIKE GOING to a formal dinner: you have to be dressed properly. There is no such thing as the "best equipment" for every diver, because of individual preferences and differences in sizes and shapes. But you should have the proper kind of equipment before diving. Try various types of equipment in diving shops before making a purchase. Consult an experienced diver and a certified underwater instructor. Since water pressure and conditions have an important effect on the fit of a faceplate or fins, fit should be the primary consideration.

It is difficult to classify any single item of equipment as the most essential, since the lack of any of several different items will greatly impair your underwater efficiency. Therefore each item should be given special consideration.

First, we'll consider the needs of the snorkel diver—a mask, snorkel, fins, and flippers.

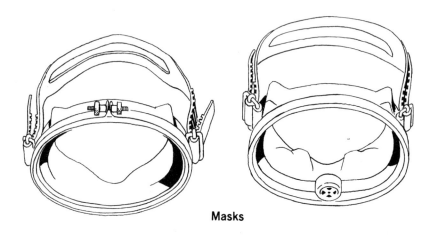

Masks

Mask

Your face mask is your magic window to the sea. The human eye, normally close to being blind underwater, can see clearly if an airspace is locked between it and the water. The modern face mask consists of a shatterproof glass faceplate in a soft neoprene or rubber skirt and made watertight by a stainless metal band surrounding the edge. The skirt is flexible enough to accommodate the specific contours of your face. Masks made of less pliable material, such as plastic or hard rubber, should be avoided, for they usually allow some water to enter through smile or eye wrinkles on the face.

Face masks whose plates are made of plastic or tinted glass should also be avoided. Plastic has a habit of fogging and obscuring vision, and tinted glass diminishes the intensity of light transmitted to the eye. Since light decreases in intensity the deeper the diver goes, there is little point in risking still further decrease by using a tinted faceplate. Goggles that cover only the eyes also have serious drawbacks, not the least of which is that they distort vision unless they are perfectly aligned. Furthermore, there is no way to equalize pressure between the two eyepieces. These problems of vision and pressure equalization don't exist with the single plate of glass now used almost universally.

A rubber strap around the diver's head holds the faceplate in place. But this strap should be adjustable, not part of the skirt in which the plate lodges. If you place your mask in position and inhale slightly through your nose, the mask should remain in place without the head strap. This is a good way to test your mask for proper fit and for the possibility of leaks before you buy. With the strap on, the mask should fit comfortably on your face without irritating or leaving red marks.

The faceplate lens should, of course, be of totally transparent safety glass affording the widest possible angle of view. There should be no curvature of the lens, since the added peripheral vision does not compensate for the increase in distortion. If you wear the proper faceplate, objects in the water will appear closer than they are and about one-fourth larger.

Snorkel

The snorkel is a J-shaped tube made of plastic or hard rubber. One end is equipped with a soft rubber bit that fits into your mouth, and the other end extends into the air, allowing you to breathe surface air while your face is submerged.

After inhaling, you exhale sharply through the snorkel to eliminate any accumulated water. However, it is impossible to completely clear the snorkel tube of all water. The intelligent diver inhales very slowly, so that residual water remains in the snorkel, and exhales sharply. With a little practice, you will find this routine easy to master. No energy is wasted lifting your head in and out of the water to inhale and exhale, and you will find you can cruise along the surface like this for long periods without becoming exhausted.

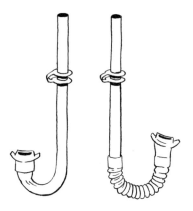

Snorkels

Some snorkels come equipped with closure devices that fit on the open end. They usually consist of a ping-pong ball in a cage. Other snorkels contain a purging valve that is meant to keep the tube dry. However, these devices often function improperly and can prove more of a liability than an asset. The ideal snorkel is the J-shaped open-end tube with a soft-rubber mouthpiece that will not irritate the gums or teeth. The tube should measure from 16 to 18 inches, for anything longer might make proper breathing a chore. The diameter also should be wide enough to allow the free passage of air adequate to your needs; the larger you are, the larger the diameter should be. If the diameter is too wide, however, it will be increasingly difficult to clear the snorkel of water.

Fins or Flippers

A fin or flipper is a rubber shoe with a rubber paddle attached. Fins provide an extra area on the feet, giving more impetus to a leg kick and helping you propel yourself through the water. A diver equipped with fins is much more versatile: the fins are doing the swimming work, and the diver's hands are free to handle equipment and game. It should be emphasized that fins are not meant as a means to help non-swimmers venture into deep water. They are designed to assist swimmers. Even good swimmers unaccustomed to the extra strain fins place on the legs may experience leg cramps while diving. Make sure, therefore, to practice with the fins on before attempting to dive with them.

There are two types of fins in common use—open-heel fins and full-foot fins. The latter type fits over the entire foot like a shoe and is superior to the open-heel fin that simply fits over the front of the foot and is secured in place by a heel strap. If you use open-heel fins, secure your foot into the fin before pull-

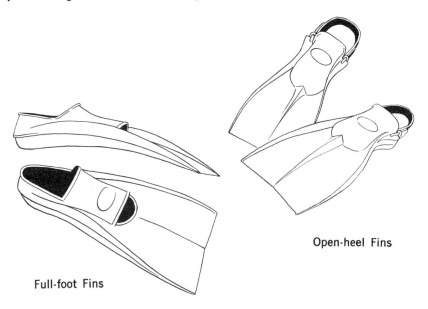

Open-heel Fins

Full-foot Fins

ing the strap over the heel. If too much strain is placed on the strap it may break. Many divers wear diving boots in conjunction with open-heel fins for added protection.

As we have noted, the fit of the fins is extremely important.

If they are too tight, they may cause cramps, blisters, and fatigue. If they are too loose, they may chafe and can be easily lost. Fins lost in the surf are a common mishap for divers. That is why fins with adjustable heel straps are not recommended. The buckle often fails to function correctly and the strap breaks.

Now that you're dressed for diving, you'll need two added accouterments for outside your person that no diver should be without. They are some form of flotation equipment and a diving flag.

Floats

As an aid to the diver in reaching the diving spot from the shore, to carry game or equipment, and in an emergency, as a passive lifesaver, floats are an essential item. An anchor line attached to a float will prevent it from blowing or drifting away. This line can be attached to seaweed or rocks and will save you much time and effort in chasing an un-anchored float. When diving in areas where no seaweed or rocks are available for anchoring your float, it is recommended that you take down a substantial line attached to your float. This will keep the float within a safe distance.

Paddle Board

Surfmat

The most commonly used type of flotation equipment is the inner tube. These are low in cost and readily available. However, you should be certain that any inner tube you use is in perfect condition. Synthetic rubber is the best material. Many divers construct their own fish nets by attaching a long gunny sack to the center of their inner tubes. This net enables the diver to place his game catch out of the water when he wishes to maneuver over seaweed or otherwise move more easily through the water.

The advantage of the surfmat as a float is that it can be propelled much faster and is more sturdy. A strong quarter-inch length rope should be securely attached to the brass "eye" rings with which most mats are equipped. The rope provides the diver with a handle for attaching the game sack and other equipment.

Another flotation device is a paddleboard, of which there are many types. The one most commonly used for diving is two feet wide and six feet long. The front is rounded and the back is square. This board is usually constructed of balsa wood and is covered by fiberglass. A hole, usually 10 inches in diameter, is cut into the front center, enabling the diver to kick along the surface and view the bottom by placing his faceplate above the hole.

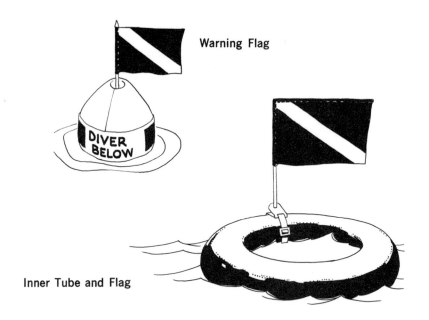

Warning Flag

Inner Tube and Flag

Diving Flag

The diving flag, usually called a "Diver Down" flag, is an essential item for a diving expedition in an area where boat traffic may be expected. The flag is square with a red background and a diagonal white stripe, one-fifth the size of the entire flag, extending from the top of the hoist to the bottom of the flag. The flag is hung above a float when the diver is swimming any distance from shore. A 12-inch square flag is flown from a one-man or two-man float; a 21-inch square flag is recommended for boats up to 40 feet in length, and a 33-inch square flag is recommended for boats up to 80 feet in length.

In addition to the basic underwater garments divers commonly wear for diving, many enthusiasts also wear suits covering their entire body to protect themselves from scratches and to cut down cold water circulation next to the skin. These suits are particularly in vogue among divers who go much deeper than the skin divers, equipped with snorkel equipment, we have concerned ourselves with thus far in this chapter.

Dry Suit

Dry Suits

Divers of the past wore woolen sweaters and pants to protect their bodies from scratches and to retain body heat. Now suits made of rubber are in wide use. They are called exposure suits, of which there are two basic varieties—dry suits and wet suits.

The dry suit is made of a thin rubber or plastic, which itself is not a good heat insulator, so undergarments must be worn inside. Wool is an insulator if it is kept dry. When the dry suit is worn over woolen underwear, the combination of the two provides good protection for the diver. The overall efficiency of the dry suit depends on its ability to keep water away from the diver's body, thus maintaining an insulation between the body and the outer layer of rubber and plastic. If the suit has a break, or doesn't fit properly, water may enter, both destroying the protection against cold and causing a marked change in buoyancy.

Wet Suits

In recent years it has become such a costly process to produce a reliable dry suit that manufacturers have nearly stopped mak-

Wet Suit

ing them. The dry suits still produced for the popular market are not nearly as reliable as the wet suits, which are more effective, cheaper, and easier to maintain.

Almost all wets suits are made of foam neoprene. The reason these are called wet suits is that they *allow* water to enter. The suit is made to fit snugly next to the diver's body. Because foam neoprene is known to tear easily, most wet suits also have a backing of synthetic non-deteriorating cloth such as stretch nylon for added strength.

The most traumatic moment for a diver wearing a wet suit occurs when the layer of water seeps inside the suit, creating a sudden upset in the diver's comfort. However, once the suit fills with water, the water is trapped there. It cannot circulate and carry off body heat, and the body very quickly warms the thin layer of water to body temperature. Insulated at this point not only by the foam neoprene, which is excellent as an insulator because it contains thousands of tiny nitrogen bubbles, but also by the thin layer of body-warmed water, the diver can travel in cold water in relative comfort. However, the addition of a neoprene hood will ensure the diver's complete protection from the cold.

Because of the free passage of water inside and outside the wet suit, water pressures inside and out are always the same. Therefore there are never any problems of suit squeeze as there sometimes are with dry suits. Because of the required skin-tight fit of the wet suit, the diver should always have one custom-made to his specifications. The suit should also be equipped with zippers at the arm, leg, and chest openings. Even then the diver's entry into the suit may be difficult unless the interior of the suit is sprinkled with talcum powder before it is worn, thus assuring that the material will slide over the skin without bending or tearing.

Wet suits require a certain amount of care, which can add

years to the life of an individual suit. After each ocean dive, the suit should be rinsed thoroughly in fresh water and allowed to dry slowly in the shade, because sunlight is known to be harmful to neoprene. Then the suit should be sprinkled liberally with talcum powder and stored in a cool, dark place. In storing the suit, it is advisable to roll it up, rather than hang it up, because the natural weight of the suit will create stress at the point where it passes over a hanger, resulting in premature damage.

Gloves

Gloves

In addition to a protective suit, it is highly recommended that you wear some type of gloves when you go underwater, to protect your hands from abrasions caused by sharp rocks and shells, and from stings from worms and other sea life. Cheap leather work gloves are suitable for this purpose, and almost any type of glove is better than none.

Gloves will also enable you to pick up in your hands any objects you may encounter underwater, such as shells and the like, without risking injury. Of course, in order to find these specimens, it is first necessary to have specialized tools for the purpose. Among these tools are spears, prying tools, and knives.

Prying Tools

Since spearfishing is by far the most popular form of underwater hunting, an entire chapter of this book is devoted to it (Chapter 6). But we shall discuss the other implements here. Almost any strong iron, steel, or aluminum bar can be used as

Prying Tool

a prying tool. A strong screwdriver is also satisfactory. The implement should be from eight to twelve inches in length and slightly curved. Though the tool should be chisel-edged at one end, making it convenient for prying loose seaweed from a hole, or digging out shells from a crevice, the chisel edge must not be sharp.

Knife

A sharp, sturdy diving knife is an indispensable aid to a diver and is actually more important as a tool than a weapon. Whether you are interested in hunting underwater or not, you should always carry a knife with you, preferably one of heavy construction with a thick blade made of stainless steel. A non-corrosive material like stainless steel is important, because salt water has a deteriorating effect on other materials. Plastic and rubber may be used for the handle.

Your knife should be serrated on one edge to enable you to cut through rope. The other edge should be straight, to allow you to cut your way through underwater lines or seaweed. Only a fool would pit his diving knife against an oncoming shark in the manner many Hollywood creations have depicted. The knife should be carried in a safety sheath to allow you to avoid bodily contact with the blade. Keep it handy at all times, worn on your belt or strapped to your calf.

Now for the actual scuba equipment itself. There are two primary types of scuba equipment, closed-circuit and open-circuit. However, the closed-circuit variety is not recommended for sport divers. It is meant only for professional divers. It is used often in military operations since the absence of bubbles floating to the

Knife and Leg Sheath

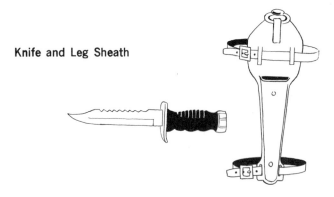

surface makes it impossible for an enemy to detect that divers are present below.

Open-circuit scuba is the established type used by sport divers all over the world. Basically, all open-circuit scuba are the same. They utilize a high-pressure air cylinder, a cylinder valve assembly, a harness, a valve for controlling the flow of high-pressure air, breathing tubes, mask or mouthpiece for inhalation, and an exhalation valve. The valve for controlling the flow of high-pressure air takes the form of an automatic demand regulator. For most sport diving the scuba should also feature a reserve air or warning device to let the diver know he is running out of air.

Regulators

Obviously, the most important scuba equipment is that concerned with the compression of air, its storage, and delivery to the diver's lungs. The regulator is the mechanism that controls the flow of air from the high-pressure cylinder to the lungs. The basic single-stage, double-hose regulator in common use today differs very little from the original model developed by the Frenchmen Cousteau and Gagnan back in 1943. This regulator consists of a non-corrosive housing divided into two chambers by a very flexible rubber diaphragm. On one side of the diaphragm is a watertight air chamber, and on the other side is a water chamber that is open to the sea. A corrugated rubber hose leads from the air chamber to the diver's mouth, and from his mouth it returns to the water chamber.

Within the regulator, the air pressure on one side of the diaphragm is always equal to the water pressure on the other side. When the diver inhales he creates a slight vacuum in the air chamber. To fill this vacuum, the water must push against the diaphragm, activating a lever that opens and closes a valve. This valve regulates the flow of air from the air cylinder. When the diver's lungs are full, the vacuum ceases to exist, the water and air pressures are again equalized, and the diaphragm returns to its normal position, thereby releasing the pressure on the valve-activating lever, and closing the valve.

At this point the pressure of the air inside the regulator air chamber, and inside the diver's lungs and throat, is in perfect balance with the pressure of the water around him, regardless of depth. For this reason, the diver is never aware of any squeeze from the water pressure. When the diver exhales, the air passes through the hose into the water chamber of the regulator via a one-way valve that prevents the water from entering. From there the exhaled air rises to the surface in the form of bubbles.

There is one disadvantage in this kind of single-stage regulator: the air flow begins and ends rather abruptly. This is by no means true in the case of a mechanical failure. On the contrary, the valve will remain open and provide a continuous flow of air until the cylinder is empty. But engineers have developed a two-stage regulator which has separate systems for both stages of pressure reduction.

For the occasional sport diver who is unlikely to become involved in the arduous tasks that commonly befall the professional,

Single Hose Regulator

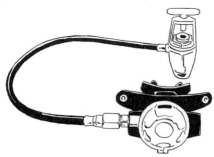

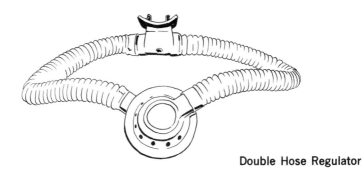

Double Hose Regulator

the two-stage regulator is more expensive than necessary. More ambitious divers who expect to achieve greater depths, and who hope to perform strenuous tasks, might consider the two-stage regulator, which can deliver greater volumes of air at greater pressures. The price of this model, however, can be as much as double that of the single-stage regulator.

Air Cylinders

Unless properly understood and handled, an air cylinder or tank can be a dangerous piece of equipment. This heavy steel item contains air under pressure. In fact, the air pressure inside the cylinder is so great that tanks are manufactured under strict regulations of the Interstate Commerce Commission. By law, the pressure rating of each tank is stamped on its shoulder near the valve, together with the date of its last pressure test. It is illegal to charge an air tank beyond the pressure rating stamped on it, because if a tank is charged too far beyond its rated capacity, it can explode like a bomb. In addition, the strength of the steel cylinder weakens with time and use, because of pressure and oxidation.

For this reason, the Interstate Commerce Commission requires

Single Cylinder

that all air cylinders be **subjected** to a pressure test every five years, and a new pressure rating given if required. Because of the weakening of metal by oxidation, it is recommended that you purchase an air tank made of galvanized steel or one that is coated inside and out with a protective layer of enamel.

Air tanks come in various sizes and capacities. The most popular type is commonly called "the 71." It contains 71.2 cubic feet of air compressed to fit inside the cylinder at a pressure of 2250 pounds per square inch (P.S.I.). This is large enough to enable a man to spend 50 minutes of "down time" in the water at a depth

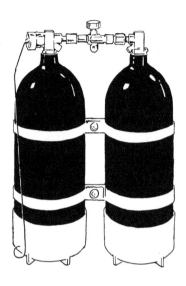

Twin Cylinders

of 33 feet. This type of cylinder weighs 39 pounds, light enough to be carried with relative ease by most male divers.

Women often prefer the 50-cubic foot tank, which is lighter, yet still holds enough air to allow a long stay on the bottom. Smaller individuals—children and beginning divers—would do well with an 18- or 24-cubic foot tank, which contains enough air at 1800 pounds per square inch to facilitate instruction sessions and brief stays below. The maximum weight of these tanks is 26 pounds.

Since all air cylinders are manufactured subject to rigid specifications, any brand you buy will be uniformly good. You should select the best tank for you on the basis of its weight, pressure rating, capacity, the type of air valve it has, the type of harness, the size of the neck opening, the protective finish, and, of course, the price.

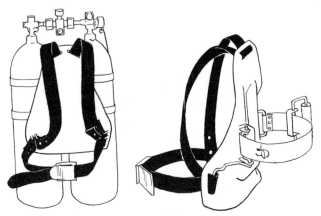

Single Cylinder Harness   Twin Pack Harness

Air Valves

The Interstate Commerce Commission requires that all air valves have a safety-release plug that will blow off at a pressure considerably lower than that which would cause the tank to explode. Two kinds of air valves are commonly used with air tanks. One is the straight K valve, a simple open-and-close mechanism

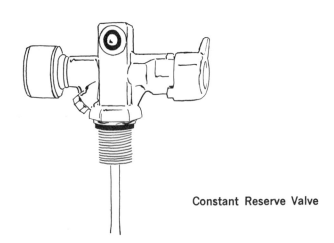

Constant Reserve Valve

that provides air direct to the regulator from the cylinder. There is no built-in air reserve mechanism; as the level of air within the tank gets lower, the more difficulty you experience in breathing. When the air pressure inside the cylinder finally reaches the level of the water pressure outside, it becomes impossible to breathe, but the diver can ascend, causing the air in the tank to expand, and allowing him more air to breathe. Once having begun his ascent, however, he cannot again descend until he has surfaced and replenished his air supply. The K valve is cheaper than the other common variety, but is not recommended for depths beyond 30 feet.

The J valve is certainly the more versatile of the two valve types. An air tank that comes equipped with a J valve is able to provide a constant reserve of air. When the air pressure drops to about 300 pounds per square inch, a spring-loaded shut-off device automatically stops the air flow. At that point the diver pulls a lever that releases the remaining 300 pounds per square inch of air pressure for breathing, and the diver knows that he has between five and fifteen more minutes—depending on his depth—of remaining air to reach the surface.

Unlike the tank with a K valve, the J valve tank allows the diver to go deeper to disentangle himself from lines or to leave the interior of a wreck or cave before ascending to the surface. Though the J valve costs approximately three times more than the K valve, the greater versatility of the J valve makes the added cost worthwhile.

A large variety of harness and back-pack assemblies are available to hold the air tank on your back. However, the ones that are sold with the tank as standard equipment are usually the best. In any case, the whole arrangement should be made of plastic, nylon, and stainless steel, to resist the corroding effects of salt water. Make sure that your harness is equipped with a quick-release buckle, so you can shed the pack should trouble arise.

Weight Belts

If the human body consisted entirely of solid tissue, the question of buoyancy would never come up. Because of the air cavities in the body, such as nose, lungs, throat, and sinuses, the body tends to float. A diver wishing to descend to the bottom could do so only with great effort—or with weights to counteract his natural buoyancy. If you are wearing a neoprene wet suit, the kind discussed earlier in this chapter, the suit itself, depending upon its thickness, might displace as much as 20 pounds of water. Therefore, you would have to carry 20 extra pounds of weights to counteract the buoyancy of the suit alone.

Pearl divers of olden times customarily carried large stones to make their task of reaching the bottom easier. Today's modern diver wears a belt with lead weights attached. By adding or subtracting the number of weights you carry on your belt, you can adjust your buoyancy until it becomes almost entirely neutral; that is, you will tend to sink when you exhale, and float when you inhale. In this manner, you are able to rise or sink with a minimum of effort. You will need added weight when diving in salt water, because it is more dense than fresh water.

Most commercially produced weights are made of lead, because it is the cheapest and heaviest material available. The standard sizes for weights are one, two, three, and five pounds. The weight belts are almost always fashioned from nylon and are equipped with a safety buckle so that a weight or weights can be quickly released with one hand in case of an emergency. This is why the weight belt must be put on last, after all other equipment is on— so that it can be removed first. The weight belt should fit snugly around the waist and not droop. The weight in the belt should fit comfortably, flat against the body, and not cause projections that can become entangled in seaweed. Remember, *never* wear weights under your suit or your scuba harness.

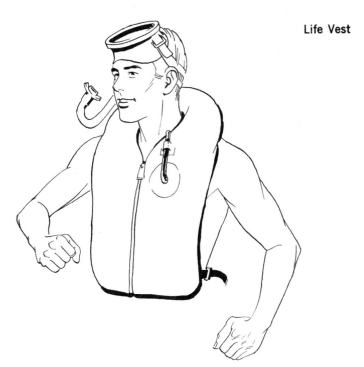

Life Vest

Life Vests

One of the most underrated forms of equipment a scuba diver can wear is a life vest. Many divers scoff at the idea of donning this emergency floatation gear. But it is an essential part of any serious diver's equipment. The chances of your needing it are remote, but it makes good sense to pack a life vest anyway. Once put on, the vest should not be taken off and used as an ordinary float, in the manner of an inner tube. In all instances, the vest should be regarded as a safety aid, and never as a substitute for good swimming skill.

Most vests operate with a small cartridge of compressed carbon dioxide which inflates a bladder made of rubber or rubberized

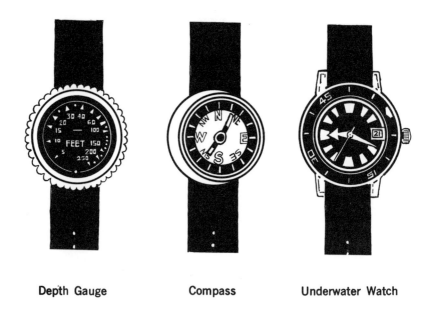

Depth Gauge   Compass   Underwater Watch

fabric. A life vest may not be very comfortable when it is inflated, but it keeps you afloat. A periodic check of the carbon dioxide cartridge should be made to investigate the possibility of a mal-function in the vest. The best types of vests can be orally inflated. A quick rinse in fresh water after use will prolong the life of any life vest.

There are other mechanical pieces of equipment that are of great use to all scuba divers. They are the pressure gauge, depth gauge, the underwater compass, and the underwater wristwatch. The skin diver may make use of any of these items, but their primary value is to the scuba diver. There are so many types of each of these accessories that the advice of an experienced diver should be sought before you purchase anything.

Pressure Gauges

The best type of pressure gauge to use is a detachable one that clamps onto the mouthpiece of the air valve in the same manner as the regulator. The pressure gauge is used most often before a dive, and reveals how much air is in the tank, thereby telling the diver how deep he can dive and how long he can stay at the bottom.

Depth Gauges

The depth gauge is useful if you wish to go lower than a depth of 33 feet. It is worn on the wrist like a watch, and the pressures are calibrated on the dial face in feet of depth. All depth gauges are equipped with a small port through which water enters and leaves. Since salt water has a corrosive effect, it is essential that your depth gauge be rinsed thoroughly in fresh water after each dive, and that the port be kept free of salt and corrosion.

Underwater Compass

An underwater compass, worn on the wrist, is used by divers who expect to have to navigate underwater. Very often, if the diver is swimming in murky water, he may find it difficult to tell one direction from another. The compass is usually suspended in a liquid-filled housing for easy visibility. The dial face should be as large as possible to make for more accuracy and easier reading.

Underwater Wristwatch

The underwater wristwatch is one of the best types of time-pieces anyone can own. It has big, bold, luminous numbers, and can be worn anywhere, in or out of water. Since all underwater watches are pressureproof, they can be used at depths of several hundred feet. Most underwater watches also contain a movable time-elapsed recording mechanism, or bezel, which records the elapsed time of a dive.

Equipment and Price Ranges

As in all activities, diving entails a certain amount of expense in the purchase of equipment. Here is a list of items useful to divers and their price ranges, based on 1970 figures:

Face masks—$3 to $15
Snorkels—$3 to $10
Fins—$6 to $15 (open-heel); $9 to $20 (full-foot)
Inner tubes—$8 to $13
Diving flags—$7 to $10
Wet suits—$60 to $90
Hoods—$8
Gloves—$8 to $13
Boots—$7 to $10
Regulators (single-stage, double hose)—$75 to $100
Air tanks—$70 to $120 (71.2 cubic feet); $60 to $100 (50 cubic feet)
Air valves—$20 to $75
Harnesses—$15 to $30
Weight belts—$5 to $10
Life vests—$25 to $35
Pressure gauges—$10 to $30
Depth gauges—$5 to $40
Knives—$5 to $15
Underwater lights—$10 to $20
Underwater compasses—$3 to $15
Underwater wristwatches—$50 to $100

4.

Basic Diving Techniques

OBVIOUSLY, THE MOST IMPORTANT thing you must do to become a skin diver is enter the water. This may sound funny, but it is a matter to be regarded seriously. Many people who have a natural fear of the water will find it impossible to ever overcome their fears. As we mentioned in Chapter 2, it is not completely necessary that you be an accomplished swimmer before attempting to dive, but it will help if you possess certain aquatic skills and know how to handle yourself in water.

Furthermore, there is another step between learning about your equipment and entering the water with it. That step is learning how to put on and use your equipment. You should practice using each item of your equipment before making any serious dives, so that you will become accustomed to the "feel" of the various objects on your body.

You will notice, for example, that walking with your fins on can be very awkward. You must lift your feet high off the ground to prevent the blade of the fin from buckling and tripping you. When you begin walking into the water, you will notice that the blade

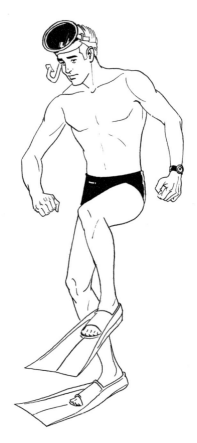

Walking on Land

will constantly buckle under you from the resistance of the water. Because of this, you may prefer to enter the water backward, to lower the surface area of the fins affected by water resistance.

Before entering the water, there is a special process involved in getting your mask ready for diving. It is called defogging the mask. The warm moist air from your exhalation will collect on the faceplate of your mask unless it is defogged before you enter the water. You defog your mask simply by spitting on the inside of the faceplate, and then rubbing the saliva all around the glass. Scientists still cannot explain why the contents of your saliva create a shield that will prevent moisture from collecting on your faceplate and obscuring vision. There are commercially produced solutions you can use for defogging your mask, but your saliva will work fine and has the great advantage of being free of charge.

With your mask defogged and your fins securely in place, you can enter the water and lower your head underneath the surface when the level of the water has reached a few inches above your waist. Bend at the waist and submerge yourself to the level of your ears and practice breathing through your snorkel. You will notice that, even though you are not totally submerged, the water pressure will press the mask close to your face, creating a tight seal. You will also discover that no water is able to leak around the snorkel in your mouth.

While you practice breathing, try to get into the habit of inhaling slowly and exhaling strongly. This will clear the snorkel

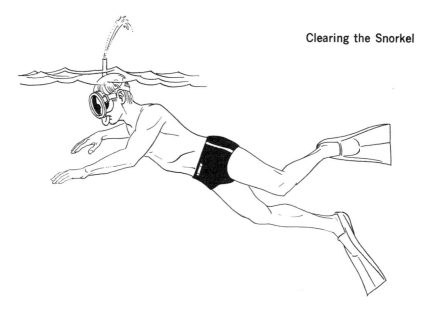

Clearing the Snorkel

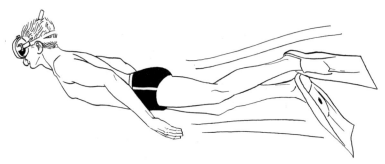

Underwater Kick

tube of any water that may leak in through the open end above your head. Try breathing through your snorkel while floating on the surface of the water and pressing yourself lightly against the bottom or hanging onto a friend's hand to keep yourself afloat.

Once you have become accustomed to breathing through your snorkel, you should hang onto the edge of the pool or onto someone's hand and stretch out so that your body lies flat on the surface. Keeping your face submerged, practice kicking with your flippers, using the flutter kick you should know from the basic crawl stroke in swimming. Keep your knees straight, point your toes outward, and kick from the hips.

Because of the large surface area of your flippers, it requires more effort to move your legs through the water than it would if they were naked, so you may notice that your legs will quickly grow tired. This is not unusual for new divers. Swimming requires the individual to make use of both his arms and legs, but diving becomes essentially an activity of the legs. You will want your arms free to carry equipment, such as a camera or a spear. Therefore, you should concentrate on developing your leg muscles to the point where they can accept the strain that long periods spent kicking with the flippers will place on them.

When practicing kicking, remember that your fins must remain submerged or you will lose a good percentage of the power and efficiency of your kick. By slightly raising your head, you will lower your feet so that each fin will remain submerged when you kick. You will soon learn that you do not have to kick as rapidly with your fins on as you would be compelled to do without them. A strong, steady pace of about twenty kicks per minute will allow you to cruise through the water at a good rate without inviting fatigue.

Feet-First Dive

As you develop this ability, you will realize how really super-fluous your arms are to diving. In fact, the movement of your arms while cruising will simply create added drag that will slow you down. Practice keeping your arms pinned to your sides, so that you will become accustomed to not having to use them.

You can also cruise by using the dolphin, or porpoise kick, in which both legs sweep up and down simultaneously.

After you have developed the technique of cruising on the surface, you may wish to move on to diving from the surface. The best method for this is the *feet-first dive*, which is used to great advantage by spearfishermen, but which is highly recommended for all divers.

You begin the dive from a vertical position in the water. Kicking your flippers powerfully, raise yourself out of the water up to

Dolphin Kick

Head-First Dive

your chest with a downward stroke of your hands and feet. Your weight above the water will assure complete submersion. Bring your arms sharply upward as you descend, and the force of this movement will enable you to drive yourself further beneath the surface. Once you are underwater, roll over and continue your descent head-first, so that you can have a clear perspective of the direction in which you are heading.

You may also enter the water initially by means of a *head-first dive*. To accomplish this maneuver, put your head down, bend at the hips, and throw your legs straight into the air. The weight of your legs will push you underwater. Don't begin to kick, of course, until your feet are submerged.

The feet-first method has several advantages. For spearfisherman a feet-first entry is usually more quiet than the head-first entry, and therefore the fish are less likely to be alerted to the intrusion of the diver. Secondly, a diver entering feet-first is not as likely to overshoot his objective, which sometimes happens to head-first divers. And, of course, a head-first diver may bump his head or mask on something in shallow water where the depth is not known.

As you progress further and further with snorkel equipment, you will reach a point of proficiency where the next logical step will be to don scuba equipment. Here, some of the same rules about familiarizing yourself with your equipment apply. In fact, there are few people on earth who feel more initial discomfort than a fully-dressed scuba diver before he enters the water. Besides being uncomfortable, he is usually feeling clumsy and hot. Therefore, it makes sense to get in the water as quickly as possible once you don your scuba gear.

Feet-first diving is common to scuba diving, and is often one of the most tiring aspects of the entire sport, as you can imagine, considering the amount of equipment you carry beneath the water with you. For a scuba diver to execute a feet-first dive, he will usually stand erect on the deck of a boat and, after confirming that he has a clear landing area and enough water beneath, will simply step out into space, entering the water vertically. Before making the plunge, he should steady his face mask with one hand and the lower part of his air cylinder with the other so that it does not ride up and hit him in the back of the head.

If the water is choppy, you will probably not care to enter by means of a feet-first dive from a boat that is lurching in several different directions at once. You can then choose the *back roll-in*

Side Roll-in Entry

entry. You execute this by facing the middle of the boat and sitting, back to the water, as close to the edge of the gunwale as possible. After steadying your mask and air cylinder as explained above, simply lean back over the water until the weight of your tank pulls you in. In very rough water, you may prefer the *side roll-in entry,* in which you crawl up to the gunwale or edge of the deck on all fours and fall sideways into the water, steadying your mask and tank before entering.

Leaving the water is not as simple as entering it. You will probably be very exhausted after a dive, and it is no easy task to pull yourself onto a deck or a boat while wearing heavy diving equipment.

You may use a deep, sturdy boarding ladder to solve the problem. A cargo net or piece of knotted rope also will help a diver climb back to the surface. In any event, you should rid yourself of as much as your heavy gear as possible before leaving the water.

While clinging to a ladder or rope, remove your weight belt and your fins, since the latter may buckle beneath you on one of the steps of the ladder. You may also remove your air tank if it feels too heavy to carry out of the water with you, especially if the boat is rocking. You can hand over all equipment you remove to a friend on deck.

Just as we described earlier in the chapter dealing with methods for learning how to use your snorkel equipment, there are some good ways in which you can learn to make use of your scuba. Standing in waist-deep water, put your mask and mouthpiece in place and submerge your face. While hanging on to a friend, practice breathing through your scuba. Don't be alarmed if, like most people, you discover that it seems impossible to either inhale or exhale the instant your face hits the water. Your conditioning has for years convinced you it is impossible to breathe while underwater; it is a belief that is difficult to dismiss.

However, once you begin believing that your scuba will enable you to breathe normally, you will find that the ability to breathe underwater is not restricted to fish. In fact, when the sensation of breathing underwater begins to feel more natural to you, you may have to resist the impulse to go swimming off in every direction. Instead, practice breathing for a while by ducking your head deeper underwater and walking your hands down a friend's leg until you reach his ankles. Then just hang on and breathe. Once your breathing becomes natural and is no longer tense or labored, you can let go and begin heading still deeper. If you are diving with an experienced partner or an instructor, swim alongside him on the bottom for a while, until you are thoroughly accustomed to the sensation.

After this exercise, you should return to the surface, and practice making dives from that point, just as you would in snorkel diving. As you proceed, you can make deeper and deeper dives. There are certain problems involved in deep diving, problems concerning both descent and ascent, that should be carefully studied before any diver can be said to be prepared. In the next chapter, you will learn about the nature of these problems and how they are solved.

First, a brief look at the laws of physics pertaining to diving seems in order. Diving physics may be briefly defined as the compression, absorption, and expansion of breathing media as related to the physiology of the body. All divers must understand and obey the laws of physics as they relate to diving, particularly the actions of gases and liquids on the body.

The main components of air are proportioned approximately as follows: nitrogen, 79 percent; oxygen, 20.94 percent; carbon dioxide, 0.03 percent; other gases (hydrogen, helium, argon, etc., 0.03 percent). Normal air is a simple mixture of all of these and is highly compressible, a factor of great importance to sport divers. Here are the properties of some of the major components of air:

Nitrogen is the major component. It is odorless, tasteless, and colorless, In a free state, at atmospheric pressure, it is chemically inactive and incapable of supporting life. Under high pressure, it is intoxicating.

Oxygen, also colorless, odorless, and tasteless, is the major breathing medium needed for life. It can be used as a substitute for regular air in some instances, but can cause oxygen poisoning when breathed for too long a period in its pure state under pressure.

Carbon dioxide is colorless but has an acid taste and odor in high concentrations. It is a combination of two parts oxygen and one part carbon and is produced by burning organic material and by oxidation of food in the body. It is the by-product of respiration, and unless excess amounts are exhaled and the gas prevented from entering the bloodstream, there may be serious reactions.

Carbon monoxide is colorless, odorless, and tasteless, but also

DIVING PHYSICS

DEPTH (in feet)	AIR AND WATER PRESSURE (in pounds per sq. in.)	TOTAL DIVING TIME WITH STANDARD COMPRESSED AIR TANK (approximate)
SEA LEVEL 0	14.7 (1 atm.)	1 tank=90'
33	29.4 (2 atm.)	½ tank=45'
66	44.1 (3 atm.)	⅓ tank=30'
99	58.8 (4 atm.)	¼ tank=23'
132	73.5 (5 atm.)	⅕ tank=18'
165	88.2 (6 atm.)	⅙ tank=15'
198	102.9 (7 atm.)	⅐ tank=13'
231	117.6 (8 atm.)	⅛ tank=11'
264	132.3 (9 atm.)	⅑ tank=10'
297	147.0 (10 atm.)	⅒ tank=9'

AIR DURATION FOR EACH 10 FEET OF DEPTH

DEPTH	MINUTES*
0	90'
10	69'
20	56'
30	47'
40	41'
50	36'
60	32'
70	29'
80	26'
90	24'
100	25'
110	20'
120	19'
130	18'
140	
150	
160	
165	15'
170	
180	
190	
198	13'

ZERO DECOMPRESSION LIMITS

No decompression necessary

Beginning of decompression table →

DEPTH (in feet)	MAX. TIME (in minutes)
35	310'
40	200'
50	100'
60	60'
70	50'
80	40'
90	30'
100	25'
110	20'
120	15'
130	10'
140	10'
150	5'
160	5'
170	5'
180	5'
190	5'

End of zero decompression limits

* Not computed for temperature change, and for descending and ascending time allowance

** Not to be exceeded within a 12-hour period

WATER TEMPERATURE

Above 75° F.—No special suit
60-75° F.—Woolen underwear
30-60° F.—Wet or dry suit
Below 30° F.—Comb. of wet and dry suits

DIVING HAZARDS

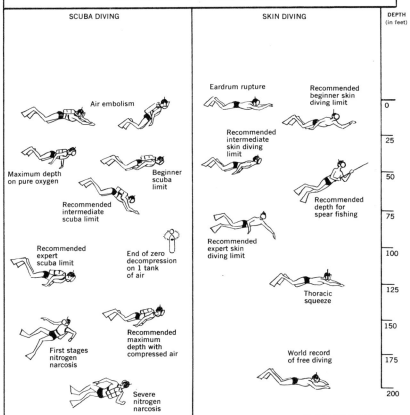

| SCUBA DIVING | SKIN DIVING | DEPTH (in feet) |

Air embolism

Eardrum rupture

Recommended beginner skin diving limit

0

Recommended intermediate skin diving limit

25

Maximum depth on pure oxygen

Beginner scuba limit

50

Recommended intermediate scuba limit

Recommended depth for spear fishing

75

Recommended expert scuba limit

End of zero decompression on 1 tank of air

Recommended expert skin diving limit

100

125

Thoracic squeeze

First stages nitrogen narcosis

Recommended maximum depth with compressed air

World record of free diving

150

175

Severe nitrogen narcosis

200

Oxygen poisoning with compressed air

BOYLE'S LAW—its practical application in scuba diving (The volume of a gas varies inversely with the pressure, if temperature is constant).

$$P_1V_1 = P_2V_2 \qquad V_2 = \frac{P_1V_1}{P_2}$$

P_1 = 1 atmosphere pressure at surface
V_1 = volume of compressed air, in cu. ft.
P_2 = pressure at a given depth
V_2 = volume of air needed at a given depth

Problem: Air duration at 66 ft. (3 atmospheres pressure). One 72 cu. ft. tankful = 90 minutes at surface

$$V_2 = \frac{1 \times 72}{3} = 24 \text{ cu. ft.} \qquad \frac{24}{72} \times 90 = 30 \text{ minutes}$$

Answer: At 66 ft., one 72 cu. ft. tankful supplies air for 30 minutes.

*Since temperature change is negligible, it is not considered in the formula.

highly poisonous. It is produced by the oxidation of carbon-bearing substances and is found in dangerous amounts in engine exhausts. Any breathing of even small amounts of this gas under pressure is hazardous and can prove fatal.

Air has weight, occupies space, and exerts force. The air surrounding the earth exerts a force of approximately 14.7 pounds per square inch at sea level. The word "atmosphere" is used to denote this pressure.

Whenever a gas, or combination of gases, is enclosed in a container, be it air cylinder or lung, it exerts pressure. The behavior of the gas is affected by varying conditions of pressure, volume, and temperature. The way they vary are part of the basic laws of physics, Boyle's Law, Henry's Law, Dalton's Law, and Charles' Law.

Before defining these laws, let us note that for practical purposes, the weight of fresh water is 62.4 pounds per cubic foot, and the weight of sea water is about 64 pounds per cubic foot. Since it is virtually impossible to compress water, the pressure which it exerts is in direct proportion to its depth. This weight of sea water is .445 pounds per square inch for every foot in depth. At 33 feet a total pressure of approximately 14.7 pounds per square inch is exerted. Each additional 33 feet of sea water also exerts an additional pressure of 14.7 P.S.I. However, when considering pressures in diving, the surface air pressure must also be considered. Therefore, all references to pressure at a given depth in the sea must include atmospheric pressure and represents the total ambient pressure at that point. This is called *absolute pressure*.

When the surface atmospheric pressure is not considered, and only the underwater pressures are mentioned, this is called *gauge pressure*. This is the pressure measured by your depth gauge.

Boyle's Law deals with the contraction and expansion of gases due to pressure. It states that at a constant temperature, the volume of a gas varies inversely as the absolute pressure, while the density varies directly in relation to the pressure. To express it in simple terms, if the pressure on a gas is doubled, the density also doubles, but the volume is cut by one-half.

This reduction in volume is one of the biggest problems a diver faces as he descends further and further beneath the surface. Fortunately, the lungs have elasticity and do not collapse under this pressure.

Charles' Law states that at a constant pressure, the volume of a gas varies directly in relation to the absolute temperature. That is, as temperature increases, volume increases, and vice versa. Since the changes in volume and the pressure of gases caused by temperature variation are usually quite small, they are not normally considered in connection with sport diving.

Henry's Law, dealing with the ability of liquids to absorb gases under pressure, has a greater relevance for divers. It states that the weight of a liquid at a given temperature is very nearly directly proportional to the partial or independent pressure of that gas. In other words, at two atmospheres of pressure, for example at 33 feet of depth beneath the surface, almost twice as much can be dissolved in a liquid; at three atmospheres, nearly three times as much; at five atmospheres, almost five times as much, and so on.

On the other hand, when pressure is decreased, gases will be released from a liquid at nearly the same percentage rate. This has a very significant meaning for divers because, as the pressure is reduced—as in ascent—the amount of gas that is held in solution in the body will decrease and this gas is released in the form of bubbles. If these bubbles are small enough, they are released through the lungs by normal breathing. However, if they should pass beyond the lungs and expand in the arteries, they can block capillaries and prevent needed oxygen from reaching the body's tissues. If this occurs in the brain, paralysis and death are possible. Expanding bubbles in the muscle or nerve tissue produce the extremely painful cramping affliction known as "the bends."

Dalton's Law refers to the partial pressure exerted by a gas in a mixture such as air. The pressure of each gas depends upon its concentration within the mixture and each gas is considered as if it alone were present—under pressure. The law states that, in a mixture of gases, each gas exerts a pressure in direct proportion to the percentage of the total gas which it represents. This has great relevance, considering the effects of heavy percentages of an individual gas like oxygen on a diver's body. For every 100 molecules of total gas at the surface, for example, there are nearly 21 molecules of oxygen. At 33 feet oxygen produces the effect of 42 percent; at 66 feet, 63 percent; at 99 feet, 84 percent, etc. In very deep diving mixtures as little as 4 percent oxygen is used to keep the partial pressures of oxygen below toxic levels.

Another principle of physics that was first discovered by the ancient Greek scholar Archimedes is the one regarding *buoyancy*. Archimedes discovered that a body so immersed is buoyed upward by a force equal to the weight of the water it displaces. To illustrate this, you can fill a washtub with water and then place a large wooden block with a known weight in the water. Some of the water will flow over the side of the tub. If all this overflow is retrieved and weighed, you can see whether or not the block will float. If the weight of the water displaced is less than that of the block, the block will sink. If the water weighs more, the block will float and is considered buoyant.

When a swimmer enters the ocean with only a bathing suit on, he is not as buoyant as a diver who enters the water with a rubber suit. The thicker the suit worn by the diver, the greater his buoyancy, because considerably more water is being displaced and water weighs much more than the suit.

Since salt water is heavier than fresh water, it has a different buoyancy factor. A diver properly weighted for fresh water will not have enough weight for salt water. Therefore, divers must adjust the weights they carry for different conditions. Also, the deeper the diver descends, the less buoyant he becomes.

The problems presented by different light conditions beneath the surface will be considered in Chapter 7, in the section on underwater photography, but it might be worthwhile to state at this point that underwater vision is affected by two physical properties that reveal significant differences between air and water: refractive index and light penetration.

Light travels in water at only three-quarters of its speed in air. This difference causes light rays to be "bent" when they pass from air into water or from water into air. The refractive index of a substance refers to the ratio of the speed of light in a vacuum to its speed in the substance. This accounts for the visual displacement of images underwater. The distortion is considerable, but is largely corrected by the use of a face mask. Still the refractive index comes into play. The distortion ratio is seventy-five percent. Objects seem to be closer and larger than they actually are.

The limited penetration of light into water is another complicating factor. Only with the sun directly overhead and a surface free of obstructions is decent visibility assured without the use of artificial light.

Regarding underwater acoustics, sound travels more rapidly in water (about 4,800 feet per second). The underwater environment is sometimes referred to as a "silent world." This is hardly the case. There are many sounds beneath the surface, deriving from waves, surf, rocks, and gravel moving with the water, boats, and even the marine life such as fish, shrimps, and crabs.

In spite of all this, however, it is difficult to communicate by use of the voice while underwater. Only about 1 part in 10,000 of the sound energy actually enters the water when speaking into an ordinary mask. The noise produced from air escaping during exhalation and speaking further complicates matters. Therefore divers have developed other means of communication underwater, some of which are described in the next chapter. Speaking diaphragms made of metal or plastic are of assistance when properly located in a mask but they usually permit conversation only across short distances at best. Another acoustical problem is that the higher velocity of sound in water and other factors render it difficult to locate the source of a sound by hearing alone.

5.

Diving Safety and First Aid

THE CARDINAL SAFETY RULE for underwater divers is never dive alone! Diving is not for the man or woman who likes to be off by himself. An overwhelming number of accidents are suffered each year by divers who "go it alone" in the water. While the float, discussed earlier, is of importance as a silent, passive "lifeguard," a diving partner or "buddy" is an active assistant in the event of an unscheduled mishap.

Remember that a diver who gets into trouble in the water endangers not only himself, but those around him. So you should select a partner whom you can trust to observe all the proper precautions when both of you are underwater—a partner who will not wander off alone in the depths. Close communication should be maintained between divers at all times, but not to the extent where one less-prepared diver becomes dependent on a partner who has spent more pre-diving hours undergoing proper training and practice.

Two divers together in the water must be mutually dependent upon each other, and secure in the belief that each has the proper knowledge and skills to react in case of an emergency. Constant communication should be maintained by means of surface conversations or underwater signals. One diver should never leave his partner at sea while he goes ashore. Accidents have no timetable.

There are very few examples outside of this "buddy system" in diving where people need each other as much as they do when underwater. This is not to say that the greater number of people involved, the better. On the contrary, experience has shown that three or more people diving together creates a situation that can

Buddy System

be classified as dangerous at best—except if each of the divers has a specific "buddy" with whom he maintains a one-to-one relationship. Obviously, then, it is better to have an even number, rather than an odd number of individuals in each diving party. In this manner, every single diver has a partner.

Proper attire is understandably essential for all divers. When diving in water below 72 degrees Fahrenheit, a protective exposure suit is recommended. Cold water reduces body efficiency as much as 40 percent and can result in a loss of coordination. Water conducts heat away from the body at a rate 25 times greater than that of air.

In many cases, a diver's ability to withstand cold will determine whether or not he wears an exposure suit. Shivering is an obvious warning that the diver is risking trouble, and he should leave the water at once and not attempt to enter again until he has been sufficiently warmed. Usually a hot shower is the best method for restoring body heat. If a hot shower is not readily available, the diver may wrap himself in a blanket before a hot fire.

The major problem with cold water is that it tends to induce fatigue quicker than warm water. Fatigue in the water is particularly serious when the diver must negotiate through a surf or current. Many divers have encountered difficulty because they were too exhausted to get back to shore.

For this and other reasons, it is usually preferable to stay close to the shore. It is also wiser to make several short dives than one long one. Besides keeping a float of some kind with you at all times, it makes good sense to relax for a few minutes before coming back if you have ventured far from shore or must return through rough surf or strong currents.

Though diving is, for the most part, a completely safe activity, there can be no getting around the very real fact that simple drowning is the single most common cause of death among divers.

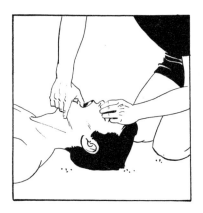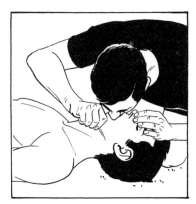

Mouth-to-Mouth Resuscitation

Panic and exhaustion within the diver are the largest factors in drowning. Since everything underwater appears 25 percent larger and closer than it actually is, a diver can easily be fooled into attempting or navigating distances for which he is not prepared.

If your partner or another diver gets into trouble, some form of flotation rescue should be attempted immediately. In the event a diver has apparently stopped breathing, artificial respiration should be tried. The mouth-to-mouth method is best, and is especially convenient on a float. Get an exchange of air into the lungs and persist as long as there is any hope for a response. Familiarity with all the Red Cross rules for mouth-to-mouth resuscitation is a big plus for any diver.

So essential is a knowledge of mouth-to-mouth resuscitation in first aid that it is used by police emergency squads and ambulance squads all over the country. Obviously it is an important procedure to know if one is going to become seriously involved in diving.

Of course, anyone who needs artificial respiration should be pulled to the surface at once. If he requires immediate attention, you may begin mouth-to-mouth treatment while still in the water; don't delay bringing him to land. If there is time, place the victim on shore, but do not change his position. Clear his lungs and air passages of water by lifting him by the midriff and shaking him. If the victim's mask is flooded, lift a corner of it up to allow the water to drain out and then replace it. Make sure that he has not swallowed his tongue by inserting your fingers in his mouth and pulling it forward. If he is wearing a snorkel tube, clear it by blowing through the open end, which should be facing you. Insert the mouthpiece into the victim's mouth and hold it shut by cupping your hand under his chin and over his mouth.

Then you can blow into the tube until you feel the victim's chest become fully expanded. Make sure that the mask doesn't ride up on the victim's face; this will allow air to escape. You must hold it down to maintain an airtight seal. If this doesn't work, remove the mask quickly and pinch his nostrils shut.

When the victim's lungs are fully inflated, relax your own mouth and allow him to exhale under his own power. Repeat the process for a full minute as fast as you can, and then resume normal breathing, blowing as hard as you can into the victim's lungs, and allowing him to exhale each time. Continue this procedure until a rescue boat arrives, but continue resuscitation as the victim is brought aboard. Mouth-to-mouth resuscitation is especially valuable in the event of a chest injury to a diver.

In extreme cases, such as electrocution, shock, and some respiratory accidents, a diver's heart may stop beating. When this happens, the tissues quickly become starved for blood and irreparable brain damage may set in within four minutes. Owing to a revolutionary method for closed-chest heart massage developed a few years ago by Dr. William B. Kouwenhoven of Johns Hopkins Hospital in Baltimore, such cases can now be treated by quick-acting divers who are fully proficient at this first aid practice.

Basically, the procedure for closed-chest heart massage is as

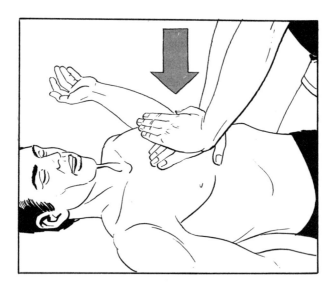

External Heart Massage

follows: with the victim's head tilted far back to prevent strangulation place your left hand on top of the right and press vertically downward so that the breastbone becomes depressed 1-1¼ inches. When treating a child, use one hand and relatively light pressure. You will note that the chest of an unconscious person is very flexible and will depress without great difficulty.

As soon as the victim's breastbone is depressed, relieve the pressure with your hands immediately. Then repeat in a cadence of 60 to 80 thrusts per minute, approximately the normal heart action.

Although Dr. Kouwenhoven's treatment has proved very successful in many cases and has been proclaimed the greatest advance in first aid since the development of mouth-to-mouth resuscitation, it is almost not worth attempting at all unless done proficiently. Only if medical attention is totally absent and not within easy access should a non-professional attempt closed-chest heart massage. Mouth-to-mouth resuscitation should be continued at the same time.

Panic is most liable to occur in a diver who is unprepared for emergencies that can occur in the water. The reaction is best described as a sudden, unreasoning fear. Loss of his reasoning powers is a luxury no diver can afford. Many divers frequently panic when they lose their faceplate, their mouthpiece, or their air supply. Yet even these conditions can be handled calmly if the diver has spent enough time underwater practicing under all conditions.

Of course, it is a considerable help in many situations if the diver possesses a knowledge of basic first-aid practices. First aid can often mean the difference between a minor mishap or a serious accident—and sometimes between life and death.

Minor cuts, abrasions, and bites are fairly common occurrences at the beach and can be attended to routinely. However, divers can sustain deep lacerations and puncture wounds or other injuries where parts of shells and sea life become embedded in the flesh. This is no longer routine. First aid must be used to stop the flow of blood. The best thing to do is to rush the victim to a doctor. But much can be done to help a victim before he sees a doctor.

All cuts and scratches should be cleaned at once to ward off the possibility of infection. Even a cut received when a diver is out of the water is subject to the same possibilities of infection when he enters the water. Among the most common types of cuts a diver may suffer in the water are barnacle, mussel, and coral cuts.

Many coastline areas are thickly populated by sharp-edged shellfish, such as barnacles and mussels. Divers can suffer severe cuts and abrasions when thrown into contact with these by wave action when entering and leaving the water. Such areas should be avoided if possible. But if you do receive a wound caused by these shellfish, cleanse it with soap and fresh water, apply an antiseptic bandage, and treat it like any abrasion.

Coral cuts are fairly common among divers who operate in tropical waters. Although they usually are not serious, coral wounds may be itchy, slow to heal, and may lead to infection. Some produce a burning sting effect that disappears almost as rapidly as it came. In most cases, coral cuts can be treated by washing the afflicted area with baking soda or a weak ammonia solution, followed by soap and fresh water. Use cortisone ointment on the wound to relieve pain.

When the pain begins to subside, cleanse the wound thoroughly with soap and water to remove all foreign matter. Then apply an antiseptic and dressing. In severe cases, as when the diver is thrown against the coral head by surf, put the victim to bed and elevate the affected limbs. Apply poultices or set dressings of magnesium sulfate or glycerine solution.

Remember, all breaks in the skin are subject to infection in or out of water. The water does *not* act as an antiseptic, contrary to popular belief.

Here again, cold water has a deleterious effect on divers. We have noted that low temperatures can fool inexperienced divers into attempting dangerous feats. Cold water also numbs the pain of an injury and may lull the diver into false complacency. Furthermore, wounds received under pressure may not bleed as freely as those received on the surface. Never overlook or shrug off any injuries received underwater.

When going on a diving trip, particularly to a remote area where medical help may not be readily available, make sure to pack a first-aid kit. Usually, the contents of your kit should depend primarily on how far you will be from medical help. Remember, first aid is simply that: a temporary form of initial assistance to a wounded diver. In no case should first aid be considered a substitute for medical attention, especially when it is obvious the injury is not a minor one.

The following items may be considered the most basic for inclusion in any first aid kit: sterile gauze squares; two-inch roller bandages; triangular bandages; a form of antiseptic other than iodine; tourniquet bandages; adhesive tape or band-aids; ammonia ampules.

Diving in remote areas where medical help would not be immediately available requires a more thorough set of first-aid supplies, such as most of these in addition to those already named: sterile bandage compresses; ointment for burns; scissors; wire or thin board splints; castor oil or mineral oil for the eyes; alcohol to rinse the ears (ear infections, common in warm or dirty water, may be prevented by rinsing the ear canal with a solution of 70 to 90 percent alcohol and water).

Despite our discussion of first aid's usefulness in diving, it is very likely that any problems you encounter as a diver will have more to do with something quite different from any mishap that would require first aid: the effects of pressure on the body. Since diving involves, more than anything else, a descent into, followed by an ascent out of the water, the problems involved in both are of paramount concern for study.

Actually, the study of the effects pressure has on the human body may best be divided into three parts: (1) effects of descent; (2) effects of depth; (3) effects of ascent.

Elementary physics tells us that compression increases as we descend further below the surface. The body is remarkably well adapted for pressure. It can withstand air pressure in excess of 30 atmospheres—a diving depth of about 300 feet—without any problem, if the normal process of breathing is not impaired.

However, when pressure on body surfaces is not applied equally, even a difference of one-sixteenth of an atmosphere—about one pound per square inch—can produce serious effects.

Among these are congestion of tissues, swelling within, and bleeding from tissues. These changes can result in pain, shock, and the destruction of body cells.

Lung Squeeze

Various parts of the human organism are affected in different ways when pressure is unequal during diving. Unequal air pressure on the lungs, best illustrated by a diver attempting to dive merely by holding his breath, subjects the diver to an extra pressure force of one atmosphere for every 33 feet of descent. At a

Lung Squeeze

depth of 100 feet—much further than almost anybody would want to go—the total pressure acting on the body amounts to about four atmospheres. At this depth, the amount of air which was present in the diver's chest at the surface—approximately 12 pints—is compressed to one-fourth that amount, or just three pints. This amount nearly equals the amount of air left in the lungs after even the most forceful exhalation. Clearly, then, at a depth of 132 feet, when the pressure reaches five atmospheres, the amount of air in the lungs reaches a dangerously low level. The chest walls and diaphragm can no longer function without stress, and a condition known as thoracic, or lung "squeeze" occurs.

The effect of the squeeze is to force blood, swollen tissue, and fluids into the spaces in the lungs normally occupied by air. The damage to the lungs at this point is considerable, and can prove fatal. In fact, if at this point, the diver descends still further, death will be immediate because the chest walls will be completely crushed.

Sinus Squeeze

We have cautioned individuals with sinus conditions against diving. This does not mean people with no previous sinus problems will be able to dive without exercising some caution. Sinuses —there are four different pairs—are cavities in the bones of the face and head. They are lined with a membrane continuous with that of the nose, running through the canals which connect the sinuses to the nose.

If the membrane swells up, it may shut off the sinus completely. This is common when one has a bad cold, and in many cases people are never able to equalize properly. These people would be ill advised to attempt diving at all.

Trying to take pressure when your sinuses won't equalize properly is asking for a good case of sinusitis, or sinus squeeze. Sometimes nose drops or similar medication will clear up the situation, but it is wise to refrain from further diving if sinus squeeze has encroached.

Middle-Ear Squeeze

A more serious problem is middle-ear squeeze. The middle ear is completely sealed off from the outside ear canal by the eardrum. The middle ear space is rigid-walled and connects to the nose area through the Eustachian tube. This tube is about 1½ inches long, and extremely narrow. The function of this passage is to allow air to pass freely from the middle ear to the nose and throat. Should the passage become blocked, preventing the free exchange of air, a difficult situation may occur.

The problem is that the Eustachian tube doesn't always pass air very readily. The diver may have to simulate yawning, or perform swallowing and other jaw-moving maneuvers to get the tube open. A few people have voluntary control over certain muscles and can open it at will. But most of us aren't this fortunate. It may even be necessary to grab your nose and blow hard to get air started through. However, if you blow too hard the passage may shut even tighter.

Because of the presence of a cold, infection, or hay fever, some people may never be able to "pop their ears" properly. The use of nose drops, spray, or inhaler may alleviate this problem, but again it is urged that you do not endanger yourself unnecessarily by pushing yourself too far. If you have been unable to equalize pressure by getting air through the tube, and descend still further, the blood vessels in the middle ear will begin to dilate. Since the membrane lining continues over the inner surface of the drum the blood vessels in the drum expand or enlarge also.

The vessels are not designed to absorb great pressure and the differential will squeeze a lot of blood into them. Just how far they go depends on how severe the squeeze is and how long it lasts. When they begin to leak, the fluid part of the blood oozes out and causes swelling of the membrane. A more intense squeeze will cause the vessels to burst, and result in actual bleeding into the tissue. If swelling and bleeding continue very long, the membrane will be "blown up" and start to peel off the body wall. Before this has gone very far, the surface of the lining will break and blood will flow directly into the middle ear space.

If the squeeze is sufficiently severe, the eardrum will rupture during this process, causing intense pain. It takes only a few feet of descent without equalization of the middle ear to cause discomfort, and as little as ten feet of such descent to cause a rupture of the drum. Without infection a rupture may be cleared up in a couple of weeks, but medical attention is essential if anything but minor discomfort is experienced in the ear.

Nosebleed and Face-Mask Squeeze

Less serious problems that may arise during descent include nosebleed, face-mask squeeze, and pain in the teeth. Nosebleed may occur as a result of a squeeze on one of the sinuses. The only treatment is to avoid pressure changes for a day or two.

Face-mask squeeze is a condition that arises when the air pressure within the diver's face mask is less than that of the external water pressure. The depth at which it will occur depends largely on how much air is in the mask when the diver starts his descent. As he descends, the air in the mask is reduced and the water pressure forces the mask lens up against his nose. This discomfort can be alleviated by slowly exhaling through the nose into the face-mask.

Teeth Pain

Pain in one or more teeth may suggest the presence of a small gas pocket in the pulp or in a part of the tooth where soft tissue can be squeezed. This pocket may lie under a filling, inlay, or cap. If the pain is severe, diving should be discontinued at once and not resumed until a dentist can remove the gas pocket.

Nitrogen Narcosis

In addition to the problems that descent may cause, there are specific problems caused by *depth* of descent. One, of course, is drowning. Others are nitrogen narcosis—known more commonly as "rapture of the deep"—oxygen poisoning, and carbon dioxide poisoning.

"Rapture of the deep" may have a romantic sound to it, but it is actually anything but romantic. When the body is exposed to pressures of four atmospheres or higher, the nitrogen intake produces an effect similar to that induced by anesthesia. The diver's ability to think clearly and to work effectively is dulled, almost as if he were under the effects of alcohol. When overtaken by the "rapture," a diver may gradually begin to lose his sense of self-preservation, become irresponsible in his actions, and operate under a general feeling of euphoria which can be extremely dangerous. Although physiologists are not exactly certain why this occurs, there is a feeling that nitrogen, a relatively heavy gas, prevents proper exhalation of carbon dioxide from the lungs and forces the body tissues to retain more carbon dioxide than normal.

The effects of narcosis don't begin to tell until about 100 feet of depth is reached. Only expert scuba divers should venture beyond 100 feet. The absolute limit for even the most experienced divers would appear to be about 300 feet, since even an expert may be unable to perform normally at this level. The only way narcosis can be corrected is for the diver to return to more moderate depths, at which time the senses return at the same rate at which they were numbed. There is no after-effect.

Oxygen Poisoning

Since oxygen is essential to life, and large amounts of it are beneficial in many types of disease, many people find themselves unable to accept the fact that oxygen can prove harmful in many ways. For divers, the potential harm of oxygen is one of the most important lessons to be learned and remembered. Even at the surface, prolonged breathing of 60 percent oxygen can cause harm, usually in the nature of lung irritation. This is rare because the air normally contains only 20 percent oxygen. For patients in oxygen tents, the range of increased oxygen usually never goes beyond 60 percent.

A diver using pure oxygen is confronted with a danger caused by the increased pressures he encounters at increased depths. Below 33 feet, high oxygen concentration within the body produces serious changes in the nervous and muscular systems. Nausea is the symptom most frequently encountered. A striking and more serious effect of oxygen poisoning is a convulsion resembling an epileptic fit. When this occurs, the scuba diver runs a great risk of drowning.

Other symptoms, dependent largely upon the depth and the condition of the individual, may include dizziness, blurred vision, shortness of breath, restlessness, irritability, anxiety, numbness, and a "pins and needles" sensation. A period of time normally elapses before any symptoms occur, but there is a high degree of variance for both this time period and within individuals, so no precise depth limitation can be set. However, it is usually wise for a diver using pure oxygen to avoid descending beyond 30 feet.

Carbon Dioxide Poisoning

With the exception of headache, drowsiness, and laziness, which may continue for several hours following seizures, symptoms of oxygen poisoning normally disappear rapidly. Carbon dioxide poisoning, however, may have a more lasting, and therefore, more serious effect. It is essential that a limit be placed on the amount of carbon dioxide intake.

At surface pressure, the amount of intake a person can experience without stress is less than three percent. If this pressure

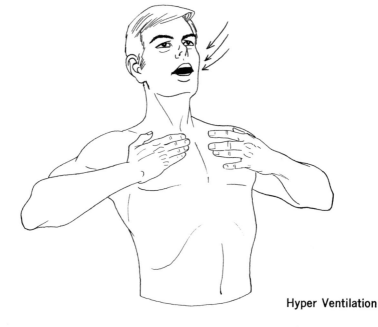

Hyper Ventilation

is allowed to increase, it increases the breathing rate. Under such conditions, the diver will become exhausted, not only from his labored breathing, but also from the poisonous effects of the carbon dioxide that he has accumulated within his body. Any attempt to continue to work under these circumstances only aggravates the condition, because more carbon dioxide is produced by the exercise involved. In addition to the basic problems of carbon dioxide, it has also been found that it increases the poisonous potential of oxygen and the narcosis of nitrogen. A high incidence of "bends," which we shall consider, has also been associated with a rise in the carbon dioxide level. Other symptoms that may indicate carbon dioxide poisoning include anxiety, nausea, excessive perspiration, and dizziness. Severe cases can result in cyanosis—a condition in which the skin turns blue due to lack of oxygen in the blood—and even death.

Divers can control the amount of air inhaled or exhaled by a method of forceful breathing called *hyperventilation*. This deep breathing provides additional supplies of oxygen and hastens the elimination of carbon dioxide. Hyperventilation is useful to skin divers, but should *never* be used by scuba divers. Breath-holding is essential to a skin-diver. It determines the length of time he can remain underwater without breathing apparatus. The scuba diver, who goes underwater with breathing apparatus, should never employ breath-holding because of the danger of air embolism and the possible buildup of carbon dioxide in the body.

Hyperventilation, with the emphasis on exhalation, will build up an extra supply of oxygen within the respiratory system. Breathing pure oxygen before a dive increases the breath-holding time below the water even further, but this can be extremely dangerous under certain conditions, as we have seen, and has caused unconsciousness and even death.

Obviously, the over-use of hyperventilation and breath-holding can be dangerous. The diver should not use them to excess. For the most part, skin divers who make their normal short dives with normal deep breathing in between will prolong their diving time most safely and enjoyably.

Air Embolism

Probably the most serious problems for any skin diver are those that can confront him when he is ascending. It is absolutely essential that he master a knowledge of ascent technique because the consequences for not doing so can be ominous. For example, there is the danger of an air embolism, caused by overexpansion of the lungs. An air embolism is one of the most frightening maladies that can occur during diving. The conditions producing air embolism are directly opposite to those which cause lung squeeze during descent.

If a diver ascends while holding his breath, the air within his lungs will expand. Since there is no way of disposing of this excess air, pressure is built up within the lungs that is greater than the pressure surrounding the diver's chest. This pressure overexpands the lungs and ruptures the air sacs and blood vessels.

The real danger in holding one's breath during ascent is that the diver need be ascending only a few feet without regular breathing for an embolism to take place. Only a slight increase in pressure in the lungs will force air to enter into the ruptured and torn blood vessels and cause bubbles to enter the capillary buds of the lung. From there they are carried to the left chambers of the heart and into the arterial blood vessels where they produce various symptoms of circulatory blockage to the heart, brain, spinal cord, and other vital organs. The interruption of the flow of oxygen-carrying blood results in the breakdown of brain tissue. If the situation persists beyond four or five minutes the damage to the brain can be fatal.

Treatment of air embolism involves recompression—as soon as possible—in a pressure chamber, where the air bubbles are diminished in size. If the duration and severity of the symptoms are not too great, recovery is possible. However, death may result in severe cases, even after prompt treatment in a pressure chamber.

We have already pointed out that breath-holding should never be attempted by anyone using scuba, and especially while rising to the surface. Air embolism can occur in as little as six feet of water, during a very slight ascent, or even in a swimming pool. It is essential to continue normal breathing during ascent. The only indication that the lungs may be expanding too quickly is a sensation of discomfort behind the breastbone and a slight feeling of actual stretching in the lungs. It is also urged that the diver not ascend too quickly. A good rule to follow is that you never overtake the bubbles (from the exhaust) or exceed 60 feet per minute when ascending.

The Bends

The other common problem involved in a diver's climb to the surface is caisson disease, more usually known as the "bends."

We have seen that when a person dives, he enters areas of different pressure conditions, and that the pressure of nitrogen on the blood is increased. When this takes place, more and more nitrogen goes into solution in the blood. A certain amount of nitrogen is always present in everyone's body tissues and blood, and varies greatly among individuals. But in diving situations, when the blood carries the increased nitrogen to the body cells, which are also under pressure, the nitrogen content of the cells also increases. Only normal breathing can eliminate this excess nitrogen, and it is a slow process, varying directly with the depth, time underwater, and the circulatory efficiency of the diver.

The nitrogen must be thrown off during ascension. Since the pressure will decrease during this time, the blood will hold less nitrogen in solution. Because nitrogen is eliminated slowly, the diver must allow time for his climb and must not attempt it too rapidly. The interval allowed for ascent is called the *decompression* time. If this period is not suitable, the blood and tissues approach a state of super-saturation; that is, they contain more dissolved nitrogen gas than they are capable of holding in solution.

When the human body contains dissolved nitrogen at a pressure twice that of the outside pressure, bubbles are formed in the bloodstream and tissues. The bubbles evolve more quickly than the lungs can eliminate the excess gas. This is the same phenomenon that occurs when a bottle of soda is opened and a deluge of bubbles rush to the top.

A heavy accumulation of nitrogen bubbles in the blood and tissues can create serious circulation blockage, destruction of brain tissue, and depending upon their proximity to vital organs, convulsions, paralysis, asphyxiation, and strangulation. Stiffness and soreness of joints and muscles, and an itch or rash of the skin are more typical symptoms in milder cases.

The only treatment for this malady is recompression—forcing the nitrogen back into solution and then, using a much longer decompression time, return the diver to atmospheric pressure.

At the first signs of illness, the diver should be placed in a recompression chamber. Time is essential, because permanent damage may result if the "bends" achieve an advanced stage.

The location of the nearest recompression chamber and the swiftest method of reaching it should be known to all divers using scuba. However, if decompression is necessary and the diver runs out of air before or during decompression, he may surface, take another scuba, and immediately return to the proper depth without taking time to change any gear. For this reason, a diver should always have a spare scuba ready for use should any of his dives require decompression time.

Decompression times are established so that the nitrogen pressure in the tissues never exceeds twice the pressure of the outside water. Bubbles will not form within this two-to-one ratio. Because of this, a scuba diver may ascend at any time from within 33 feet of depth, regardless of exposure time—at a rate of not more than 60 feet per minute. Susceptibility to "bends" varies greatly among individuals, and to some extent within a single individual from time to time. Age and exertion are other factors in a diver's susceptibility.

The United States Navy has developed a standard decompression table which is in common use by most scuba divers. The table and instructions on how to make use of it are offered later in the volume. The Navy has never made claim that the table is foolproof. Obviously, the table cannot foresee every possible diving situation, nor can it allow for the wide varieties in individuals making use of it, and the different types of conditions under which dives are made. Furthermore, the decompression table cannot in any way be construed as a guaranteed prevention of or treatment for air embolism or bends.

The Navy developed the table with these facts in mind. It was considered better to encounter, and treat, an occasional case of bends or embolism, rather than to use a perfectly safe, but impractical table. Diving to the exact lengths and times specified in the table may produce evidence of decompression sickness up to five percent. The point scuba divers must remember is this: even when following the table to the exact specifications, divers may experience decompression sickness. The fact that the table has been violated without serious consequences on rare occasions can best be attributed to good fortune and to the low susceptibility of the individuals involved. It is best not to even come close to the limits set by the table, but to play it safe by using a depth-time level considerably lower than the maximum.

There are other medical problems that can be encountered in the course of diving. A brief summary of the most serious and common ailments follows:

Cramps

This particular condition can be caused by overworking of underdeveloped muscles, extreme heat or cold, and diving too soon after eating. A muscle or group of muscles will contract involuntarily and cause great pain. If cramps occur in the water, firmly press the affected muscle and work the pain out with gentle massage. Apply heat to the affected area as soon as possible for quick relief.

Carbon Monoxide Poisoning

The contamination of a diver's air supply by carbon monoxide fumes frequently results in carbon monoxide poisoning. It can be prevented by always making certain that your air supply is certified pure. Symptoms include unconsciousness, headaches, weakness, clumsiness, and confusion similar to drunkenness. The lips, fingernails, and skin turn reddish in color, and in severe cases breathing may stop. Victims usually recover rapidly with exposure to fresh air, but may suffer lingering after-effects, such as headaches and nausea.

Emphysema

There are two basic types of emphysema—subcutaneous, in which escaped lung air lodges in tissues just beneath the skin, causing a swelling and usually occurring in the neck and collar-bone areas; and *mediastinal,* in which the escaped lung air collects in the tissues surrounding the heart, major blood vessels, trachea, larynx, and other parts of the body. Though neither type of emphysema is very serious by itself, the presence of either kind may indicate the presence of an air embolism. The symptoms are similar and treatment should take the same form as for air embolism.

Pneumothorax

The presence of air pockets between the lungs and the walls of the chest cavity, which can cause collapse of a lung and extreme difficulty in breathing, results in the condition known as pneumothorax. This may be another sign that an air embolism is present. If not, it is not necessary to recompress. But immediate medical help should be sought and oxygen administered.

Shock

Shock is usually the result of a traumatic injury or any condition that causes a loss of blood or body fluids. When it occurs, the body cannot keep its blood pressure up and tissues are starved for oxygen. Unless treated quickly and correctly, death may ensue. The bleeding can be stopped by applying a tourniquet between the wound and the heart. Loosen the tourniquet every half hour for five minutes. The victim should have his head lowered and his limbs elevated. He must have a transfusion of blood or plasma as quickly as possible to replace lost blood. If the victim is conscious and not vomiting, he should be fed a mixture of one teaspoon of table salt and one-half teaspoon of baking soda.

As in all areas of diving, the individuals who make the soundest use of the equipment they inherently possess, and by which they are surrounded, are the happiest divers—and safest. No amount of equipment of instruction can compensate for good, sound judgment and knowledge of safety techniques.

Here is a point-by-point summary of safety tips that every diver must know:

> Never dive alone. Always bring a partner and use the "buddy system."
>
> Always use a diving flag to communicate with others in the water.
>
> Make sure your diving attire is suitable for the weather and water conditions around you.
>
> Don't overextend yourself with too much diving, or with dives of long duration.
>
> Use a safety hitch or quick-release buckle on your harness and weight belt.
>
> Keep some sort of float with you at all times.
>
> Pack a suitable first-aid kit and bring to diving a basic knowledge of first-aid techniques, particularly artificial respiration and the treatment of cuts.
>
> Know the symptoms of the major pressure illnesses.
>
> Never hold your breath when using scuba.
>
> You should also learn the following hand and line pull signals as a means of communication beneath the water.

In Chapter 4, it was pointed out that voice communication is virtually impossible between divers, except across close distances. Therefore divers must rely on other means of communication. Over the years a standard set of signals has evolved and is widely used throughout the world. Visual signals by hand are the most practical in average situations and are the most extensively used. Of course, these can be used only when there is visual contact between two or more divers. They are inadequate in dirty water.

Line pull signals are used between divers and surface tenders during deep diving or when visibility is poor between two or more divers and contact is made by "buddy lines" connecting the divers.

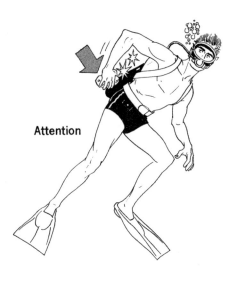

Attention

Up

Air Supply Low

Everything Okay

Look

Help Me

Hold Still

Regarding Question
of Depth or Time

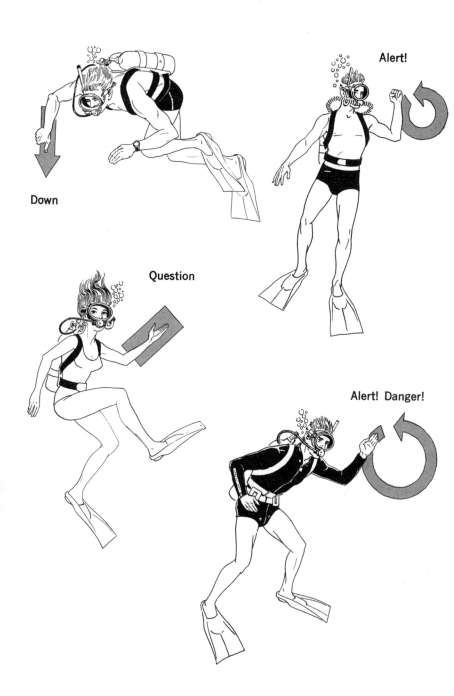

Down

Alert!

Question

Alert! Danger!

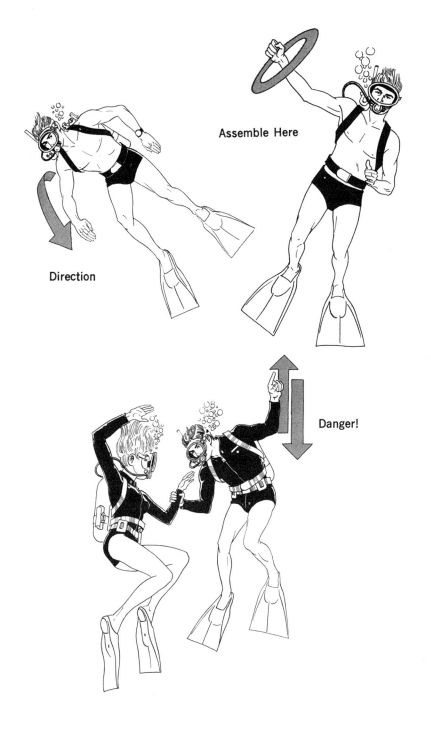

Assemble Here

Direction

Danger!

ASCENT AND DESCENT (CODE: 4–2 PULLS)

Tender to Diver		Diver to Tender	
1 pull	OK?	1 pull	OK! Proceed.
2 pulls	Going down or stop and redescend.	2 pulls	Lower away or give slack.
3 pulls	Stop. Stand by to come up.	3 pulls	Stop. Take up slack.
4 pulls	Come up.	4 pulls	Take up.
2-1 pulls	I understand but wait a minute.	2-1 pulls	I understand but wait a minute.

LIFTING AND LOWERING (CODE: 2–4 PULLS)

1 pull	Stop.	1 pull	Stop.
2 pulls	Slack off.	2 pulls	Slack off.
3 pulls	Take up slack.	3 pulls	Take up slack.
4 pulls	Haul away.	4 pulls	Haul away.
5 pulls	Line coming.	5 pulls	Send me a line.

SEARCHING (CODE: 7 PULLS)

1 pull	Stop and search there.	1 pull	I am stopping and searching here.
2 pulls	Follow where the life line leads you or (if using circle search) circle around.	2 pulls	I am following the line (diver must keep line taut) or circling.
3 pulls	Move to right.	3 pulls	I am moving to my right.
4 pulls	Move to left.	4 pulls	I am moving to my left.
5 pulls	You are there.	5 pulls	I have found objective.

EMERGENCY SIGNALS (NO CODE)

2-2-2 pulls	(Answer only.) I acknowledge you are fouled and need assistance.	2-2-2 pulls	I am fouled and need assistance from a diver.
3-3-3 pulls	I acknowledge you are fouled but are safe.	3-3-3 pulls	I am fouled but can clear myself.
4-4-4 pulls	Come up immediately!	4-4-4 pulls	Haul me up immediately!

6.

Spearfishing

WHILE ALL DIVING ACTIVITIES fall under the classification of sport, the competitive factor we associate with the word "sport" is most evident in the underwater activity known as spearfishing. Throughout the world competitive diving for game is recognized as sport. Fish and Game Departments will usually cooperate in conducting such events. "Derbies" for largest species are conducted every year in various regions, with prizes awarded on the basis of size rather than quantity. In reply to past criticism that many sea creatures were being recklessly destroyed, minimum-size limits are now strictly enforced, as are limits on the quantity of fish taken.

Spearfishing is the ideal sport for the expert diver with the instincts of the hunt. Unlike other varieties of hunting, underwater tracking of game possesses all the trappings of mystery: until the diver has gone below, he is not always certain what species he may encounter. Unlike other forms of hunting, too, the spearfisherman must remain essentially in his own environment, since he is restricted in the amount of time he can spend underwater, while the fish he stalks are not.

Carrying the Speargun

Most countries of the world prohibit spearfishing with the aid of an aqualung. The use of an aqualung, it is felt, would result in the wanton slaughter of numerous underwater species, as it would allow the diver all the time he needed for wandering about below until he found something to kill. The snorkel fisherman, of course, must return to the surface regularly for air and must rely on his diving skill and knowledge of fish behavior to make a kill.

Before you attempt to spearfish, you must decide upon your aspirations, whether you wish to seek bottom fish, rock fish, or pelagic (open water) fish.

This decision will make it easy for you to determine what type of equipment you should use in terms of the type of speargun you will carry, and the type of spearhead you select for your spear.

There are spearguns and spearheads in every price range and for every purpose. Simple hand-held spears, used for fluke and flat fish, may cost as little as three dollars. Powerful pneumatic guns with powerhead spears cost more than $100. Between these extremes are the rubber-powered, Hawaiian-style sling guns, rubber-loading arbolete guns, spring-loaded guns, and the basic pneumatic guns.

The hand-held spear is the type anyone can manufacture easily on his own. A length of solid curtain rod, for example, makes a very effective spear. Hand spears are used almost exclusively to hunt fluke, halibut, sole, rays, and other flat fish that remain stationary and partially hidden on the bottom. The diver must simply stab the fish and then slide it up the spear. Three or four fish are usually the most that can be held on the spear at once, and when that total is reached, they can usually be slipped off into the diver's utility bag, and then he can go on for more.

The Hawaiian sling-type gun is only slightly more elaborate than the hand spear. But it is often used by even the world's outstanding spearfishermen to land fish weighing up to 300 pounds. These guns are no more than simple hand spears equipped with a rubber strap. Some divers attach the strap to a short piece of bamboo or metal tubing through which the spear can slide. Some attach the strap to the end of the spear itself. In either case, the gun works like a sling shot and requires great skill and accuracy to operate effectively.

The rubber-loaded speargun is nothing more than an elaborate Hawaiian sling. The spear fits into a rubber-loaded gun, which is equipped with a trigger catch and safety mechanism. When the trigger is pulled, the spear is ejected and the rubber loaders propel the spear.

Until the appearance of pneumatic spearguns, arbolete spearguns were the most popular with spearfishermen around the world. They are available in a variety of models, varying in both size and power, and are very useful for work at close quarters and in open water.

The spring-loaded speargun consists of a long barrel with a closed-end spring attached to the inside of the muzzle. As the spear is rammed down the barrel, the closed end of the spring is stretched out until it catches on the trigger mechanism. When the trigger is pulled, the released spring contracts and propels the spear.

Although this type of gun is quite accurate and powerful, it has the drawback of requiring constant lubrication in the springs to prevent rust. In addition, the springs eventually lose their power due to metal fatigue and must be replaced frequently.

The pneumatic speargun was invented in Spain by a famous spearfisherman named Pepe Beltran of Palma de Mallorca and is currently one of the most popular weapons used in underwater hunting. The gun consists of a chamber filled with compressed air operated by a hand pump. An air-tight piston slides the entire length of the barrel from the trigger catch to the muzzle. When the spear is rammed against the piston until it catches on the trigger mechanism, the air behind the piston is compressed still further. When the piston is released, the compressed air expands and both the piston and spear are driven down the barrel.

Spearguns

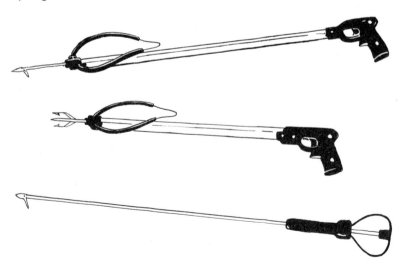

Because of the long stroke of the piston, the pneumatic gun is extremely accurate, provided you keep your spear shaft perfectly straight. One charge is sufficient to last for the entire spearfishing season, since there is never any loss of air. However, the disadvantage of the pneumatic gun is that it decreases in power the deeper you go into the water, because of the increase in water pressure. Some manufacturers have developed guns which compensate for this added water pressure, but in most cases the cost of these new models is prohibitive and the improvement minute. Because pneumatic guns are very useful in all types of situations, delivering the best combination of accuracy, power, and utility, they are the most highly recommended of all spearguns.

On most spearguns, spearheads are interchangeable. A wide variety of spearheads are available, but usually the best one for your gun is the one provided with your gun when you buy it. Most vary in price between $2 and $20. A round point does not have as much penetrating power as a point with angular sides and is not as easy to sharpen. A detachable spearhead, one that slips off the end of the spear when it enters the fish, will prevent the spear from being bent by a large snapping fish, thus saving you money for replacements.

It is important to keep your spear perfectly straight because a bent spear will not fire true. When fishing for smaller sea creatures, a multi-pronged spearhead will improve your chances for a hit and not leave a big hole in the flesh of your catch as will a standard type of spearhead.

In seeking big game, you will greatly improve the penetrating power of your spear by using a weighted spearhead. An explosive powerhead, one that fires a .22 or .32 caliber powder blank cartridge, will penetrate even very tough skins. The powerhead should be used only for large fish in open water, and then only with utmost care, for it is extremely lethal and can send the spear ricocheting back through the diver if it hits a rock or coral formation at close range.

The spearfisherman's quarry can be categorized roughly into three basic groups: rock fish, bottom fish, and pelagic fish. Rock fish take up regular residence in caves, beneath reef rocks, or among wrecks and piers, and hardly ever leave these sanctuaries. They include groupers, blackfish, eels, and the sea basses. Bottom fish, of course, are usually found on the vast expanses of flat bottom. They are usually flat fish, such as halibut, flounder, sole, and rays. Pelagic fish are always on the move, and can be described as the scavengers of the sea. All are carnivorous—meat-eaters—and they are in constant search of food. These are the jacks, bluefish, tunas, mackerel, sharks, and barracudas.

Each type of fish group contains hundreds of species, and nearly each fish within a group calls for a different stalking and striking technique in hunting it. The most experienced and best spearfishermen spend their lives studying the habits of each group, including the best times to stalk each, and what equipment to use.

The next step is to visit an area where spearfishing can be expected to be rewarding. Just as the land fisherman wouldn't waste his time fishing for trout in a stream where none are known to exist, the spearfisherman knows enough to stay away from flat sandy beaches, where, except for some bottom fish and an occasional striped bass that comes searching for food, the waters are nearly devoid of game.

Generally speaking, the best spearfishing is done around bottom areas that provide ample shelter, protection, and food for the fish who live there. These areas include holes, crevices, wrecks, jetties, piers, coral heads, and rocky headlands near deep channels. These areas are inhabited by rock fish, who are sought, in turn, by the pelagic fish who venture into the area.

The greatest spearfishing habitats in the world are coral reefs or wrecks in the warm, clear waters of the tropics. Visibility in these areas is usually one hundred or more feet and you can spend the entire day in the water without even the luxury of a wet suit.

Furthermore, you can catch a seemingly endless flow of fish of many sizes and types. The waters of the Caribbean Islands, the Florida Keys, the Bahamas, Baja California, the South Pacific, the Hawaiian Islands are ideal spearfishing locales.

Wherever you stalk fish, keep in mind that fish are among the most intelligent creatures in the entire animal kingdom. Long experience has taught them to distinguish the difference between friend and foe. They even learn to distinguish between those foes who might be searching for food, like larger fish, and those who might simply be out for exercise. Thus, the presence of a well-fed barracuda around a heavily populated reef might not be a cause for alarm among the fish in that reef. Yet, let that same barracuda make one threatening gesture and the reef fish will vacate the spot in a hurry.

Likewise, the appearance of a spearfisherman in a heavily fished area might cause the bottom fish little concern—until the hunter begins to use his spear. Then the fish may go scurrying off in all directions. Often, the exact opposite may be true. A diver may happen upon a region that has been lightly fished and the fish may come swimming at him out of sheer curiosity. If you wish, you can teach these fish to eat from your hand and even to perform tricks.

Unfortunately, however, some divers have been known to take advantage of these situations and begin killing every fish in sight to satisfy their sadistic pleasure and run up a large kill count. This may be understandable for a diver who encounters dangerous fish, like sharks or barracudas, but many divers fire spears at everything they see. These divers are the true villains of spearfishing.

If you are working in a heavily fished area—and it is very likely that you will be—you must expect your prey to be wary of your presence. The most important thing to remember is never to make quick or threatening movements or noises that can scare the fish away before you are ready to shoot. The one exception to this

reminder may be when stalking certain varieties of pelagic fish
who hole up at the sight of a diver. Very often, slapping your
hand on the surface once or twice may draw the fish out of his
hole to examine the situation. You should swim with a slow, steady
flutter kick, taking special care that your flippers do not break
the surface or cause any splashing noises.

When you spot your prey, stop moving and start hyperventilat-
ing (see Chapter 5) to clear your lungs of excess carbon dioxide
and build up the oxygen content of your blood. This will greatly
increase the time you have for your dive. When you have taken
in enough air, exhale completely. Draw in all the air you can comfortably take—and then just a bit more. As soon as you are submerged again, the increased pressure will ease any discomfort
you may experience because of the increased air.

Once underwater, bring your free hand—the one not holding
your weapon—down to your side. This will give you momentum
to help you reach the bottom. Remember, don't rush things on
your way down. Keep your kick slow and easy or you'll consume
too much energy and shorten your dive. The closer you get to
your target the better you are. Even if you are equipped with a
weapon that can shoot for a considerable distance, you are not
likely to hit a forewarned fish who is on the move beyond $1\frac{1}{2}$ spears
away. Often the fish hears the click of the trigger being pulled and
is far out of sight once the spear arrives. However, if you take the
time to stop, set yourself, and fire, and give your fish enough of a
lead, you can learn how to hit a moving target.

If the fish is holed up, take your time and draw a careful bead
before letting your spear fly. You should usually aim for the brain,
especially on larger fish, as this will kill him instantly, thereby
making impossible a struggle on his part. If you spear a fish in the
belly or in the tail, he may make a real effort to free himself, and,
depending upon his size and strength, may very well succeed.
Furthermore, his efforts may attract sharks, drawn by the sight

and smell of blood. Sharks are also the reason why you should bring all speared fish to a boat on the surface immediately, or if you are not using a boat, insert the fish into a waterproof sack attached to a float.

By far the greatest danger to a spearfisherman is the spearfisherman himself. Almost all fishing accidents are the result of foolhardy hunters who shoot recklessly or endanger themselves and other fishermen by failing to score clean kills on the fish they hit. A wounded fish may swim away, leaving a trail of blood behind him, and the spearfisherman may be accosted very rapidly by a shark.

Never forget that a speargun is a dangerous weapon, as lethal as any loaded gun. It has the capacity to kill and to do great damage. It should never be taken lightly.

7.

Underwater Photography

WHETHER it is done for pleasure or profit, underwater photography can be a thrilling test of underwater skill. It is the only way a diver can capture some of the beauty and spectacle of the sea depths and bring them to the surface for others to enjoy. At the same time, it provides a diver with a lasting record of his exciting experiences beneath the surface.

There is nothing mysterious about taking good underwater photos. All you need is a basic knowledge of photography and the special properties of underwater light, in addition to the proper photographic equipment, which consists of a camera and a special watertight housing.

There is no shortcut to photographic knowledge. If you are not an experienced land camera-bug, you had better practice taking photos above water before trying your luck underwater.

Once you're ready to take the plunge beneath, you'll quickly discover that there exists a camera and camera housing for every level of budget and proficiency. They range in size, price, and usefulness from the little box-type Brownies housed in glorified

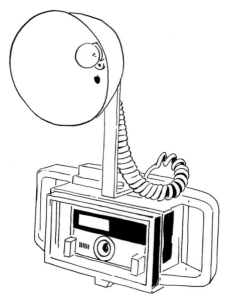

Underwater Camera and Flash

plastic bags, which sell for a few dollars, to elaborate professional motion-picture cameras in pressure-tested aluminum housings, which sell for many thousands of dollars. If these are too expensive for your taste, you can construct your own camera housing by using three-eighths inch of clear plastic for as little as $15.

If your interests run toward moving, rather than still photographs, you would do well with a simple 8-millimeter camera with a plexiglass housing. For professional-level movies, however, a quality 16-millimeter camera would be better.

The ideal underwater still camera for the average amateur photographer would be a single-lens reflex-type using a large negative (2¼ x 2½ inch or larger; 35mm. is sometimes too small to produce color reproductions of top quality), a large film load (50 to 100 exposures), a motor-driven device to transport the film, an automatic exposure setting, and a fast wide-angle lens located in a cast-aluminum case with an underwater distortion correction lens. The ideal underwater movie camera would be a 35mm. electrically-powered, self-contained underwater unit with a large film load of up to 400 exposures, and a wide-angle lens with automatic aperture setting. These cameras do not even exist except in very rare and extreme cases, where they are developed for exploration purposes by professionals. But you can have a tremendous amount of satisfaction by simply making the best use of the type of camera you do own.

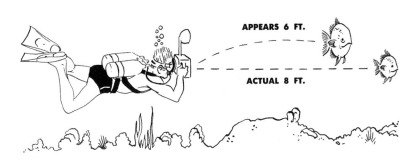

Underwater Distortion

It is essential to understand the peculiarities of light and vision under the water before taking any kind of pictures. Solar light rays diminish underwater as depth increases. At 15 feet light has already been reduced to one-fourth of its original intensity, at 50 feet to one-eighth; at 130 feet to one-thirtieth; and it vanishes almost completely at around 1000 feet. Part of the solar light is reflected back at the surface, and part is transformed into heat, but most of it is consumed by microscopic matter suspended in the water. Exactly how much light is lost in this way depends upon the density of the suspended matter.

The solar color spectrum—blue, green, indigo, orange, red, violet, and yellow—also penetrates the surface, revealing fantastic displays of color in the shallow depths. But the water itself acts as a filter on the color spectrum, and the colors also rapidly diminish in value with depth.

Some colors disappear more quickly than others; red, for example, is almost totally invisible to the naked human eye below 30 feet. It begins to appear as a deep blue beyond that point, and appears as black at greater depths. Blue, green, and violet remain visible longer than the other colors, but they, too, fade into blackness at great depths.

However, inject a fresh source of light beneath the water—such as a flash bulb—and the entire color spectrum reappears in all its original splendor. The point to remember here is that the light waves cause all objects to seem one-fourth closer than they really are. Thus an object that is actually 12 feet away appears to be only 9 feet away. In short, water magnifies.

When still in shallow depths a filter may be more helpful for accurate color balance, but any filter will cut down on the already scarce amount of available light. Below 50 feet, filters are totally impractical, as the desired red band is already absorbed by the blue-green filter factor of the water itself. It is wise to remember that no filter can restore a color, but it will balance the remaining colors to give a truer picture of what the diver actually sees.

Of course, clear water is necessary for underwater photography. Since the penetration of sunlight is limited by the clarity, density, and depth of the water, it is essential that you do not put yourself at a disadvantage from the outset by diving into murky water. The materials best suited for camera cases underwater are lucite—a type of plastic—fiberglass, or aluminum.

Lucite is the easiest to work with if you're constructing your own housing. You can see inside, facilitating setting of the controls, and detecting water leakage. Aluminum assures a heavier, more rugged housing. A round-shaped case will withstand greater pressure than a square-shaped one, even one constructed of the same material.

Any camera to be used underwater should include most of the following features: an $F/3.5$ or faster wide-angle lens; an automatic stop for each exposure; a self-cocking shutter; reflex focusing or a sound sport-type viewfinder; slightly negative buoyancy when submerged.

It is always wise to have your equipment tested for water and pressure-proof capacities before starting to use it. Most commercial housings include an air valve for the purposes of conducting this test. Put a couple of lead weights from your belt inside your housing and—assuming it has an air valve—inject a few strokes of air from the hand pump that also comes with the housing. Then lower the housing at the end of a rope into the water. If you spot air bubbles escaping, the housing has a leak. If no bubbles appear, lower the housing to its rated limit and pull it back up. If no water has penetrated the housing, you may consider it safe to pack your camera into the housing. But when placing the camera in the housing, make sure the back plate is sealed evenly on all sides so that it will not leak.

As in all picture-taking, the type of film used by the diver in underwater photography plays an important role in determining the quality of his pictures. For best results in water, the slowest possible film for each light condition is advisable. Slower film is always finer grained and produces relatively fuzzy negatives. This is true of both color and black-and-white film. Any faults created by graininess in the film will be intensified in your final prints in direct proportion to the size of the blow-up.

Since it permits greater latitude, black-and-white film is preferable over color film for underwater photography. The black-and-white films with the lowest speed are as fast as the highest-speed color films, but by using the former, you can make an exposure error of as much as two f stops and still produce a satisfactory print.

There are so many variables in underwater photography that it is always wise to experiment with different types of film, exposures, and processing to determine what combination produces the best results. If you like to do everything yourself and custom process your own work, you may purchase a very handy developing kit from your local photographic supply dealer for about $25.

The number of frustrated underwater photographers who attempt to shoot in color must be incredibly high. It's amazing how many people forget that water can do funny things to color, and that a fish or plant that looks exquisitely colorful near the surface looks despairingly drab at great depth. On deep dives, even in very clean water, the ocean floor appears to have only a dull, monochromatic color. This situation practically demands the use of an exposure meter when using color film. Remember that light is very deceptive to the eye underwater, and that you cannot correct mistakes in exposure on color film without severely damaging the color rendition.

Obviously, for many of the same reasons cited above, there is no guaranteed method for computing camera exposures for underwater *flash* photography. Experimentation is usually necessary before you can determine what will or will not work under various water and light conditions. The uncoated white flash bulbs are best for color work since the water will filter out the reds these bulbs emit and you will end up with a good balance of color.

If you use flash bulbs, which, incidentally, are practically useless at distances beyond 15 feet, even under excellent conditions, make sure to use the smaller bulbs, because the larger ones can explode in your hands when exposed to the pressure of great depths. At any rate, it is advisable to wear gloves when working with flash bulbs underwater. If you use black-and-white film, it's best to use flash bulbs only as a fill-in light.

Electric strobe lights also work well underwater, except that a red or magenta filter may be needed to compensate for the hot blue light emitted by the strobe. Unless you have had extensive practice with strobes, however, it is best not to use them underwater. They have the facility of producing high-voltage jolts which can seriously hamper your interest in underwater photography.

The best hours for shooting underwater pictures are generally between 10 A.M. and 4 P.M. It is during these hours that the sun offers its best light conditions. This does not imply that you should wait until the sun is approaching its zenith. When it is directly overhead, the sun emits a flat, monotonous light lacking in the interesting shadow effects that lend depth and variety to your photographs. For the best results, the sun should be at about 45 degrees. This is when you'll catch highlights and shadows and be able to take advantage of these effects.

8.

Catching and Maintaining Saltwater Fish

MANY DIVERS BECOME so enraptured by the spectacle they find beneath the sea that they decide to recreate parts of it in their own homes. This can be easily and efficiently done by means of a home aquarium. Maintaining an aquarium for saltwater fish isn't really much more difficult than one for the freshwater varieties you can obtain in any pet shop. Your aquarium may be all glass, or all plastic or wood with a glass front. You cannot use metal at all, because the combination of water and metal produces a reaction called electrolysis, which can burn your fish to death.

To operate your aquarium, you need a powerful, compressed air pump that can be worked 24 hours a day. The pump operates an air filter and an aerator, both of which are crucial to the health of the fish and the proper usefulness of the aquarium. The filter keeps the water within the aquarium clean, and the aerator keeps replenishing the supply of oxygen.

Another piece of equipment essential to the operation of your aquarium is a hydrometer, which measures the salinity—salt content—of the water. The average salinity rate in any salt water is

1.025, an amount that will support virtually all forms of sea life, including crustaceans. The saltwater in your local areas may have salinity as low as 1.010 or as high as 1.040, all falling within the accepted limits for the salt content of saltwater. You must watch the hydrometer to see that the salt content doesn't fall or rise beyond these limits.

The normal process of water evaporation within the tank will increase the percentage of salt in the water, an increase that will be indicated on your hydrometer. You must return the water to its proper balance by filling the tank with fresh water until the hydrometer indicates that the salinity has returned to a safe level.

A thermometer, also needed in any aquarium, will tell you what the temperature has been inside, and the water you use to replace what has been lost through evaporation should be of the same temperature. If the water is too hot or too cold, your fish will go into shock and die. The normal aquarium temperature is 75 degrees, and you should employ a heater to keep the temperature at this level.

In addition to the methods outlined for catching fish in Chapter 6, many divers like to use a slurp gun. This is an all-plastic cylinder, which operates under a plunger system. You simply point the gun at the fish and pull the plunger outward, drawing the fish into the tube by means of suction. In most cases the fish are caught unawares, They are not able to see plastic, which is invisible to them. This is a particularly useful method for getting fish out of holes or from between rocks.

Other methods employed by divers for catching saltwater fish include the baiting of minnow traps with mussels or other types of bait, and using trapping nets. Though the latter can be slow, it is really a very successful means for catching fish.

Once you have stored fish in your aquarium at home, it is a relatively simple matter to take care of their food needs. For the most part, saltwater fish subsist on a diet of live prime shrimp, and in some cases, they will eat tubifex worms. Of course, frozen shrimp, available at most supermarkets, will do fine, but you should not buy shrimp that has already been shelled and deveined. The shrimp should be bought with the shell intact so that you can take the shell off yourself.

Some specimens will eat a dry food, available in pet shops, which is very beneficial to them because it contains many vitamins not found in the natural foods. Earth worms are also an excellent food staple for saltwater fish, as are sand worms and blood worms.

During the past twenty years, many types of new saltwater fish have become common in pet shops, because divers have located these fish in different spots around the world. Nearly every pet shop owner is now able to carry a complete variety of saltwater fish. If you care to develop your own proficiency as a diver, you may even want to run your own aquarium as a part-time business. Many new divers, neither interested in pursuing fish as game, nor in recording the depths of the sea by camera, have turned their interest in fish into a profitable hobby. You may be able to sell specimens to pet shops, to other interested divers, or to fish collectors.

Of course, many divers with a genuine interest in home aquariums combine diving for their own fish with buying other specimens at pet shops. Saltwater fish are not an inexpensive item in pet shops, and the biggest reason for this is that they are very difficult to breed. If a method could be found for readily breeding these fish, their prices at pet shops would drop considerably.

Some aquariums have been successful in breeding the toad fish, a common North Atlantic species. Other saltwater fish which have been bred include clown fish and neon gobies, a widely-distributed type of fish with ventral fins united into a funnel-shaped suction disk. But for the most part, even the leading ichthyological experts have found it all but impossible to breed saltwater fish.

In short, you can make the acquisition of fish a lifelong, pleasurable hobby, and even profit by it. If you are motivated in this direction, it would be worthwhile for you to study the habitats of fish and their living habits, so that you will be able to pursue this activity with a wealth of knowledge at your fingertips. Many individuals have mastered the art of diving for vastly different reasons, but find, after initial experiences under the water, that the acquisition of sea specimens is their favorite underwater activity. It could turn out to be yours, as well.

9.

Dangerous Marine Life

AS WITH ALL VENTURES into the unknown, exploration beneath the sea has fostered many stories and legends about the life to be found there. Needless to say, many of them are fanciful and have no basis in reality.

This does not mean, however, that the diver has no reason to be conscious of dangers in the water. In fact, probably the greatest peril confronting a diver is the attitude that there is nothing to fear in the sea. This is a naive and foolhardy attitude. But if the diver takes proper precautions, and comes equipped with a good knowledge of the varieties of creatures he may encounter beneath the surface, there is no reason why he should have undue cause for concern.

In this chapter, we will discuss several of the more prevalent water menaces to man. Some, like coral and barnacles, are sedentary creatures. Others, like sharks, barracudas, and moray eels, move about freely. Still others, such as lion fish and stonefish, are quite active but are most dangerous when at rest. If these creatures are encountered or provoked under the latter circumstances, they have the potential to strike and often kill as a defense mechanism.

It is easy to say that avoiding these latter types of fish would be the wisest course of action. But this is not always possible. Because of their habitat or camouflage or strange coloring, it is often difficult to discern some of these water hazards.

Sting Ray

Sting Ray

This creature, for example, lies buried in the sand and usually springs to life only when stepped on. There are many types and varieties of sting rays, but all react the same way; when stepped on, they lash upward with the spines at the back of their tails. This may produce injuries ranging from mild punctures to lacerations of up to one inch. A spine may break off the ray's tail and become embedded in the diver's foot or any other part of the body with which it comes into contact. Even someone wading in shallow water is liable to encounter a sting ray, so it is advisable to wear foot protection of some kind.

Spiny Sea Urchin

The spiny sea urchin is always found in tropical waters, mainly in the West Indies and Florida. Each of its spines is as sharp as a hypodermic needle, and if you get stuck with one or more of these

Spiny Sea Urchins

spines, the urchin injects a black fluid into you. Sea urchins range in size from one inch to eight inches in diameter, and are probably the most common form of nuisance to divers. Jacques Cousteau, inventor of the aqualung, has said that urchins cause more painful injuries and interrupt more dives than any other form of sea life.

Once, while swimming off the beach at Nassau in the Bahamas, I (Henry Berkowitz) was chasing a spiny lobster. As I grabbed the lobster by its antennae, I was pulled into a batch of sea urchins. Fortunately, I was stuck in only one finger—I could actually see the urchin inject its venom into my finger—and was able to squeeze it out.

Coral

There are two types of coral dangerous to divers—mustard coral and fire coral. As their names imply, mustard coral is yellow in color and fire coral is red. Each will administer a severe burn when disturbed. Another form of coral, the millepore coral, found in warmer waters, can leave a rash more severe than that of poison ivy. The 1250-mile Great Barrier Reef in Australia is probably the world's most awesome coral formation.

Barnacles

One of the well-known hazards to swimmers and divers, barnacles are actually animals, a fact that is not well known. They are a variety of shellfish that grow on rocks, pilings, and tidewater areas. Sharp-edged, they can cut the diver who comes into forceful contact with them. They are particularly dangerous in tropical waters where, if a diver cuts himself badly on a barnacle or rock, there is the very real risk that sharks will be attracted by the blood.

Barnacles

Sharks

Sharks actually sense their prey, or detect when another living thing is in trouble, by means of their lateral line, a sensory organ that runs down the entire length of their body. The best procedure to follow in dealing with sharks is to treat any that are over five feet in length as potential man-eaters, no matter what kind of shark they may be. In many instances, one particular species will not bother man, but there is no reason to relax your caution on this account. When there is blood in the water, any shark may become frenzied and go after anything that moves, including other sharks.

There are actually about 300 different species of sharks, among the major ones being the shark, the whale shark, the white shark, lemon shark, hammerhead shark, sand shark, tiger shark, and nurse shark. For the most part, sharks in pairs or groups are much

more dangerous than single sharks. This is largely due to the fact
that all sharks are competing for any food possibilities that may
enter the water.

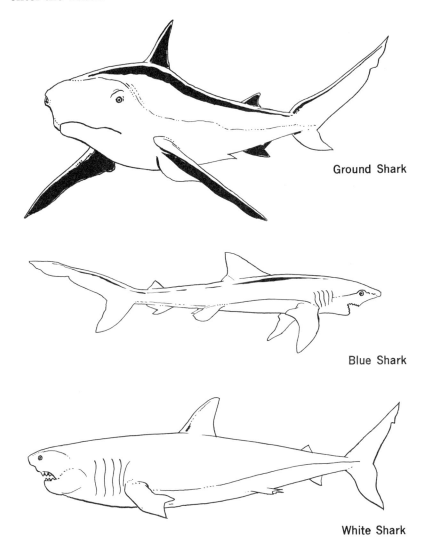

Ground Shark

Blue Shark

White Shark

An exception is the rogue shark, a species too old and weak to compete for his food in the normal manner. This type of shark usually resorts to prowling around beaches, harbors, and other places that he normally would avoid to scavenge on easier prey. Often such a shark will remain in the same area for several days because he is too feeble to move on. In fact, a rogue shark can become a regular inhabitant of an area and be given the nickname "Harbormaster" by the local populace. Many "Harbormasters" have been known to prowl the waters off Bimini.

There are many stories of shark attacks on divers and all bolster the cardinal rule when dealing with sharks: don't take chances with them. The American Institute of Biological Science has a shark research panel. The files of this committee are maintained under the direction of the Curator of Fishes. This group has mimeographed information, which it updates regularly, for people who require information on shark attacks.

Barracudas

Barracudas are very swift swimmers and usually travel in schools. They look very much like mullets, and this is not coincidental: they are in the same family. Barracudas like shiny things, and many times will go after the exposed part of the diver's

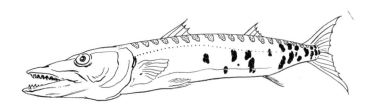

Barracuda

body, particularly the heels of the feet. One type of swim fin leaves the heels uncovered. Accordingly, when a diver wearing this type of fin kicks up and down, his heels will be exposed and relatively shiny, and could attract a barracuda. Usually, barracudas, which have long, narrow bodies and mouths crammed with teeth, measure four to six feet in length and are mostly found in Florida and the West Indies, are peaceable creatures and will attack only if speared by a diver or attacked in some other fashion.

Moray Eel

This creature dwells in tropical reefs and in crevices in the rocks and ordinarily does not strike unless cornered. It measures anywhere from six to nine feet in length, often attains a diameter of more than twelve inches, and is characterized by a small head and a wide mouth filled with rows of sharp teeth. Many divers

Moray Eel

exploring holes in reefs inadvertently place their hands into the lair of the eel. In defense, the eel will grab the offending limb with the tenacity of a bulldog. The eel has a reputation of never letting go once it has bitten. The eel's bite may also be venomous. While the animal itself doesn't contain any venom sacs, its teeth, just like those of man, can produce a venomous bite because of the chemical contents of its saliva.

Lion Fish

Another dangerous creature to watch out for, especially in Pacific waters, is the lion fish. Though non-aggressive, it uses the spines on its dorsal fin, which contain the venom of a cobra, as a means of defense. I've swum amongst them many times in Tahiti and never was attacked. They are extremely beautiful to look at, and as long as all the diver does is watch their antics in the water, he usually has no reason to fear them. But should someone try to latch onto a lion fish, he will be in for a very bad time—especially since there is no known antidote for the lion fish's poison.

Stonefish

A somewhat similar species, the stonefish, is the most deadly animal—bar none—found in tropical waters. Its deadliness is enhanced by its unique camouflage. Often, in aquariums, when stonefish are the sole occupants of a fish tank, they still are not easily identifiable because of their amazing resemblance to stones. If the eyes or the gills of the fish didn't move occasionally, one would think they were inanimate objects. The venom of the stonefish is so lethal that it can induce death in fifteen minutes. The venom is transmitted through the spines around the fish's head and gill areas. The spines are so sharp that they can penetrate tennis shoes.

Lion Fish

Stone Fish

Octopus

Next we come to the octopus, another shy, retiring creature found in all seas. There are cases, where a diver has tormented a captured octopus by dangling it around his neck, thereby provoking the creature to administer a fatal bite. Of course, the octopus also may ensnare his attacker within his eight tentacles,

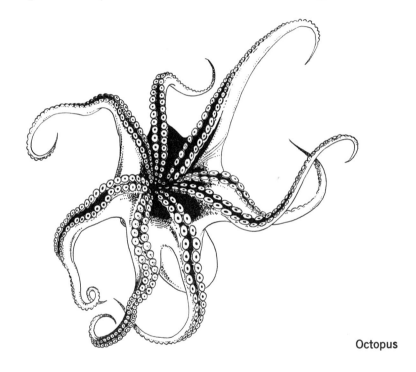

Octopus

a fate as dangerous as countless fictional accounts have reported it to be. Most octopuses, particularly the larger species, are found in the deeper regions of the sea, well beyond the area cruised by the average scuba diver.

Sea Lion

The sea lion, related to the bear family, has teeth as wicked as those of a leopard. Off the "Seal Rocks" of San Francisco, divers have been attacked by what they initially believed to be sharks. Further investigation has revealed that, in certain cases, the attacks were perpetrated by sea lions. Male sea lions, called "bulls," are extremely protective of their harems of female sea lions, and

Sea Lion

will defend them zealously. Female sea lions, incidentally, are docile creatures and almost never strike. Many sea lion breeding areas (rookeries) are found in the Galapagos Islands of the Pacific.

Jellyfish and Portuguese Man-of-War

Two closely related forms of sea life are the jellyfish and the Portuguese man-of-war. These umbrella-shaped creatures are among the simplest forms of animal life, lacking central nervous systems and many other common organs. Actually, both the jellyfish and Portuguese man-of-war are three animals in one. One animal is the float, or balloon, which makes up the top part of the entire creature; the second part is the intermediate tentacles; and the third part consists of the tentacles. These are capable of administering electric-like shocks when the diver comes into contact with the animal.

The severity of the sting applied by both the jellyfish and Portuguese man-of-war varies with the skin of the diver and the extent of the contact with the animal. Persons with light, dry skin seem to be most affected. Therefore, it is usually advisable to apply heavy mineral oil or a similar substance to the body before entering an area of water where jellyfish are known to exist. The Portuguese man-of-war has the more disabling sting of the two, but in some areas of the world there have been jellyfish whose sting was so **potent** it caused death.

Portuguese Man-of-War

Jelly Fish

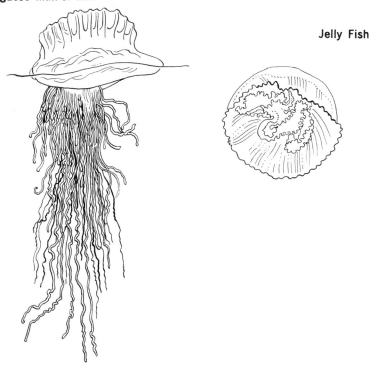

Manta Ray

Other noteworthy creatures, but types that most divers likely never would come across, are the manta ray and the killer whale. The former is dangerous only because of its immense bulk—as wide as 20 feet across from wingtip to wingtip. There have been occasions when, strange as it may seem, the manta ray has settled upon a diver, not even realizing the diver was under him. Outside of this, this ominous-looking creature, sometimes called "devil fish" because of the horn-like protrusions around its face, is completely harmless to man, since it feasts only on plankton.

Manta Ray

Killer Whale

Although the killer whale typically measures between 25 and 30 feet, not much else is known about it. There have been tales of killer whales in the Arctic region actually coming up under ice flows on which men and other animals were walking, and swallowing men and animals whole. There have been isolated instances of whales attacking small boats and even making trouble for the sea lions out in San Francisco Bay, but these are exceptional cases. Although these whales, smaller and faster than other types, have gluttonous appetites, they actually are extremely docile, as are

Killer Whale

sharks and lion fish when in captivity. In recent years people have been able to train killer whales to jump through hoops, in the manner of porpoises, and to carry their trainers on their backs, as horses do.

Kelp

There is a form of plant life that looms as a potential peril to divers, and that is seaweed, or kelp. Considered by many divers to be the ideal diving environment because of its rich abundance and various forms of sea life, intricate corridors, and colorful reactions to light, kelp's menace lies in the fact that divers can become entangled in it. When diving into kelp, a diver should carry a knife since he may have to cut his way out of it. Different varieties of kelp grow in different parts of the world's waters, but it is wise to check your proximity to its branches no matter where you are, and no matter what kind of kelp you are near.

There are several measures every diver should take before submerging that will stand him in good stead should he encounter any forms of marine life:

(1) Wear shoes when walking on eroded shores or on coral reefs.

(2) If using open-heeled fins underwater, also wear thermal socks or rubber boots.

(3) Wear gloves; they can lessen the effect of bites or stings by sea creatures.

(4) Acquaint yourself with the area in which you are diving, and the types of sea life known to be present in local waters.

(5) Equip yourself with first-aid kits that can be used in treating cuts, bites, punctures, and scrapes.

In most cases, if proper attention is given to preparations of this type, you should have little reason to worry about your diving activities. If you remember not to disturb sedentary creatures and not to place your hands into crevices or caverns where you might activate some hostile fish, you should be perfectly safe.

One very important consideration to keep in mind is not to dive in murky water. Aside from the fact that the range of your vision will be reduced under cloudy water conditions is the reality that the fish still will be able to sense *your* presence.

I have been diving for 17 years, and nothing serious has ever happened to me, aside from my near brush with a sea urchin, mentioned earlier in this chapter. And if I had taken proper precautions and avoided the spiny lobster who pulled me toward the urchin, I would be able to say I've never had any trouble in the water.

The sport of diving is extremely safe, although recklessness will occasionally take its toll. The margin for error can be greatly reduced by the application of sound judgment.

10.

Experiences of a Diver

(Narrated by Henry Berkowitz)

I SUPPOSE MY LONG INTEREST in skin diving began with my ambition to become an ichthyologist—a fish specialist. This, of course, is only one of many ways people become attached to the water. But I can remember as a boy combining my interests in art and in fish, and dreaming some day of becoming the James Audubon of fish, emulating the great naturalist who was able to paint so beautifully all he saw in nature.

My interest in the sea quite naturally led me to join the United States Navy when I became of age. By this time, my ambitions to study ichthyology had been somewhat tempered by the realities of economics. I began to study art with the intention of entering that profession in some capacity. Of course, my interest in the sea and its mysteries was still very much with me. I began to study fish and other sea life on my own. This is what led me to the great sport of skin diving. I had always enjoyed swimming, and had developed a certain amount of proficiency in it.

I decided to learn all I could about diving, and spent many hours with people whom I had befriended who were also expert divers. Unquestionably, I learned good diving technique and habits from associating with people who knew the sport well. Diving became my vehicle for catching fish and studying them— just two of the numerous thrilling activities divers can enjoy.

You have to understand the type of equipment available when I became a diver to appreciate how far the sport has come in just a short time. I began in the early nineteen-fifties, and in the ensuing years everything has changed to fantastic degrees. I used to be chided by non-diving friends for taking "risks" during my diving expeditions. In a sense, looking back on the vastly different equipment with which I started, I *was* taking risks by today's standards. But I never thought about negative factors then, and I don't think about them now. I have confidence that I know what I am doing, and this is a confidence that has come to me with experience over the years, not all of it pleasant.

I couldn't possibly participate in diving at all without the encouragement of my wife Hannah, who remained sitting on the sands of Miami Beach while I went diving during our honeymoon! Hannah, it seems, is afraid of deep water. I do not make light of her fear. In fact, I have greater respect for people who are willing to admit fear than for those who try to conceal it by doing foolhardy things. The latter individuals are a constant menace to divers; in an attempt to prove something—their masculinity, bravery, or something—these types only make it worse for truly skilled and confident divers.

As a beginning diver I was quite content just to float along the surface of the water looking at the various kinds of fish I saw. It wasn't long before I realized I could get quite close to them provided I didn't make any sudden movements that might scare them away. This isn't always a blessing.

On our honeymoon trip to Miami Beach, I went diving at every opportunity. I would swim out by a long jetty with no intention of doing anything but look around to see what I could see.

Suddenly I heard someone yelling "Shark! Shark!" at the top of his lungs.

Out of curiosity, and certainly not bravery, I asked where the shark was. Right there, someone said, pointing to a rock directly in front of me! Without stopping to think, I immediately dove until I saw the shark's tail sticking out from underneath the rock. I grabbed the tail and pulled the shark out. It was fortunate that

I happened upon a harmless shark—a baby nurse shark only about three feet in length. It had appeared much bigger underwater, and in retrospect it was foolish for me to dare to capture something I knew nothing about. But this kind of shark is absolutely harmless since it doesn't have teeth like other varieties of sharks. The teeth of a nurse shark are flat and smooth, forcing it to confine its diet to shellfish.

Of course, people at the beach thought I was a genuine hero for tackling the shark the way I did, but actually it was an unwise maneuver. Naturally, I let the shark go. About a week later we went to Nassau in the Bahamas, where I spotted a beautiful black and white moray eel. I picked up a piece of broken coral and tried to touch the moray. I followed the eel for several minutes without success. Again, I was the lucky one: had I gotten close to the moray he could have grabbed my hand and taken a few of my fingers with him.

Most diving experiences, however, involve no risk. Once, off the same jetty in Miami Beach I mentioned earlier, I was surrounded by a whole school of striped mullets. I felt as if I was driving a covered wagon in some Western movie with all the Indians closing in around me. The eyes of the fish followed me wherever I moved, and it was a very amusing sight. I couldn't keep myself from laughing, but when water started entering my face mask I had to swim out of the school of mullets to the surface.

The next day I tried the same water. Again I was quickly surrounded by fish, but these weren't docile mullets. These were barracuda! I have seen barracuda measuring eight feet long off Key West in Florida. These are really dangerous creatures. The barracuda on this particular day, though, acted in much the same way as the mullets had the day before. They swam around me, following my every move. I knew that if I tried to make a break for it, they could easily get at me. Furthermore, my heels were exposed because I was wearing open-heel fins, and the barracuda were inevitably attracted to the shiny surface of my bare heels.

Finally, I mustered up all my courage and dove right into the center of the barracuda. They quickly swam away. I was so happy and surprised with myself that I started diving all around and went under a ledge. From this vantage point I saw the most immense barracuda I had known existed to that time. He must have been about seven feet long and he was coal black in color. He was asleep when I first saw him, but he was quickly awake and saw me only seconds after I saw him. Neither of us turned out to be much in the mood for adventure; we both turned pale white and scurried away in opposite directions!

All this took place, of course, before I started carrying a spear with me. I am not an avid spearfisherman, since I prefer to take fish alive and keep them in 150-gallon tanks in my house. My first attempts at spearfishing were at Montauk Point, at the far tip of Long Island, New York.

But I have always preferred catching and keeping the fish I find in the water. In my early underwater experiences, I was content to be a sightseer. Later, I progressed to cameras with which I recorded my observations photographically. Still later, I went after fish with nets. Even today, when I enter tropical waters, I do so without a spear, because I am there only as a collector and investigator, not as a hunter.

Even in waters that are located near my home in New York, for example, off Montauk Point and Far Rockaway, I have sighted fish which were quite extraordinary. Here is where my artistic bent has served me well. I always make detailed paintings of unusual fish I encounter, and have submitted many of these to institutions such as the New York Aquarium and the Museum of Natural History. It is not unusual to spot many varieties of fish in Long Island waters, as the waters there become almost tropical in the summer. I reported many interesting observations to Dr. C.M. Breder, Jr., who then was curator of the Department of

Fishes at New York City's famed Museum of Natural History.

Usually, when I go underwater to collect fish, I take a net that has a diameter of eight inches and get as close to the fish as possible. Especially if you know the habitats of a variety of fish, you will generally be able to locate them quite easily and to prod them into your net. After a while it becomes a question of asking yourself, as I ask myself—if I were that particular fish where would I go? As far as the fish that live in reefs are concerned, there is almost no point in killing them because they are mostly inedible. But they are splendid subjects for underwater photography, and, of course, for collecting.

Perhaps my biggest disappointment as a diver came in Australia some years ago when I was in Sydney on a vacation with my wife, and naturally decided I would try diving off Australian waters.

The Bondi Beach area in Sydney has the reputation of being one of the outstanding diving areas in the world. However, upon entering the country, I had to relinquish my diving knife to the authorities because it was a double-bladed dagger knife. After that, I thought it advisable to stay out of the water, because I had become psychologically attuned—as I should have been—to having my knife with me at all times underwater.

Tahiti, on the other hand, presented quite a different experience. In fact, it was while diving in Tahitian waters that I enjoyed what was probably my greatest moment as a diver. I had the good fortune to discover a fish that was previously unknown to science—and which, to this date, still has not been identified. Diving off a Tahitian reef, I quickly found this fish living in a symbiotic relationship with a giant sea anemone. In symbiosis, two unrelated creatures live together for mutual benefit.

Before I made my discovery, the only known fish to live in a symbiotic relationship with another animal was the clown fish, which also lives in unison with the sea anemone. The clown fish acts as a lure to draw other fish into the tentacles of the anemone. The anemone then stings the lured fish to death and absorbs it, leaving the remains, or the crumbs, so to speak, to the clown fish, who is, in turn, afforded protection by the anemone.

The fish I discovered off Tahiti had the same relationship with the anemone. At first flush, I had all sorts of delusions of grandeur, that maybe the authorities would name the fish after me, at the very least. I initially reported the fish and sent a painting of it to Dr. Breder at the Museum of Natural History, who confirmed that the fish was, indeed, of an unknown species. He sent the painting on to Christopher Coates, then the Curator of the New York Aquarium, who suggested I correspond with Dr. Demorest Davenport, an expert on symbiotic relationships who is on the faculty of the University of California, Santa Barbara Branch. Dr. Davenport, in turn, suggested I contact even a greater authority, Dr. Adelbert Hackinger of Vienna. The collective genius of all these great scientists was not able to make a clear identification of the fish I discovered, and possibly the fish will remain unknown for all time.

Or maybe one of you will discover it when you visit Tahiti. Whether your interests lie in hunting, photographing, or collecting species of sea life, you're bound to have countless enjoyable experiences. You may want to do as I have done—keep a handy record of all your experiences in the water. That's one of the glories of our sport, that even an amateur can add something entirely new to science or to the lore of the sea. I have no hesitation in calling it the greatest sport in the world.

Certainly one of the most attractive features of underwater diving is that it can be practiced in so many spots both in the United States and around the world. There follows a partial listing of great diving locations in North America:

UNITED STATES

New York—Finger Lakes, Lake George, Long Island waters
off Montauk Point; and Fishers Island.

New Jersey—Long Branch, Cape May.

New England—Gloucester, Massachusetts; Isle of Shoals.

Georgia—off Savannah.

Great Lakes—Lake Erie, Door County, Wisconsin.

The Carolinas and Virginia—Cape Fear, Cape Lookout, Cape
Romain, Cape Hatteras.

Florida—Key Largo, Key West.

The Gulf States—Grand Isle, Louisiana; the Gulf of Mexico.

Desert states—Lake Mead, Arizona; Sea of Cortez.

California—La Jolla, Long Beach, Catalina, Newport, Corona
del Mar, Malibu, off San Francisco, Baja, Mendocino, Monterey.

Montana—Flat Head Lake.

Washington—Hood Canal, San Juan Islands.

CANADA

Nova Scotia—Gold River, Mahone Bay.

Quebec—Richelieu River, Lake Champlain.

British Columbia—Diver Rock.

There is also excellent diving available in many areas of the
Caribbean, including the Bahamas; Bimini, British West Indies;
Italy; southern France; Australia; and South America.

One of the great attractions of scuba diving is the allure of
treasure hunting. Many adventurous souls have been driven
underwater in the hope that they will recover fantastic treasures,
many considered long lost, lying on the ocean floor. However,
these treasures are usually more fiction than fact. Most reported
treasures never existed; they were products of the imagination,
often of just a single individual who perpetuated the myth.

Many alleged treasures have proven to be collections of spices, silks, and other perishable items that were absorbed by the sea years ago. Anyone with aspirations in treasure diving should study carefully the history of the accounts of the particular treasures in which he is interested. Divers should also plan how they will store, transport, and dispose of any items they do find, and also study the nature of any claims that may already been made on such items, and what clearance, if any, will be required to seek it.

Occasionally, the salvage of a great treasure of gold and silver sends countless new hopefuls scurrying beneath the surface in quest of new treasures, but for the most part they come back to the surface disappointed. Furthermore, even if you should locate pieces of a valuable hoard, the cost of transporting it back to the surface might not be worth the effort.

Epilogue

BY THIS TIME you are undoubtedly aware that you have joined the ranks of a new breed of pioneers, that anyone who dives beneath the sea is tapping what is as yet a largely unexplored world of mystery and adventure.

It has been little more than a quarter of a century—since the invention of the aqualung by Cousteau and Gagnan—that man has progressed beyond the dark ages of the sea. The fact that the sale of diving equipment has increased a hundredfold among amateurs and professionals alike in the ensuing years illustrates the adventurous spirit in man which Cousteau and Gagnan awakened. It is now estimated that more than 500,000 individuals in the United States alone dive annually, and that about 1,000 diving clubs are functioning in various parts of the country.

Though largely unpublicized in comparison to assaults made in outer space, the increased awareness of the sea's mysteries over the past 25 years has resulted in numerous scientific assaults on the age-old secrets that remain hidden in the depths of Inner Space.

All phases of oceanographic study and exploration have sky-rocketed in popularity all over the world. Scientists are descending to the ocean floor in ever-increasing flocks to make firsthand investigations of underwater phenomena. Research vessels, as well, have probed the seven seas in ever-increasing numbers in quest of information about the wonders of the sea.

New types of diving vehicles—and there are always different types being developed—have opened up nearly 50,000 cubic miles of untapped ocean to explore for every yard of depth attained. Worldwide cooperative efforts, such as the International Geophysical Year and the Inter-Governmental Oceanographic Commission of UNESCO, have provided nations with a marvelous opportunity to benefit from one another's discoveries.

Already, man has found numerous means to make use of the 166,000,000 tons of dissolved mineral salts found in every one of the *300,000,000 cubic miles* of ocean water. Many of these salts are turned into precious metals. Man has tapped vast mineral resources beneath the ocean bottoms, harnessed some of the sea's vast power, and learned to cultivate underwater species of life for food. He has also learned how to manufacture fresh water from sea water, and through the developing science of underwater archeology, has found the sea to be an incredible storehouse and museum of fabulous artifacts.

For example, several years ago the famous Galatea Expedition, in which oceanographers and ecologists combined their talents, investigated and brought up species of fish that had never been seen before. They resembled dirigibles in appearance, and were lacking in appendages, fins, and eyes—in fact all features but a mouth. They had the features of monsters, but were only a foot in length.

The late President John F. Kennedy recognized the importance of the sea as one solution to the physical problems facing the exploding world population. On March 29, 1961, he sent a letter to Congress, the contents of which follow:

The seas around us, as I pointed out in my message to Congress on February 23, represent one of our most important resources. If vigorously developed, this resource can be a source of great benefit to the nation and to all mankind . . . But it will require concerted action, purposefully directed, with vision and ingenuity. It will require the combined efforts of our scientists and institutions, both public and private, and the coordinated efforts of many federal agencies.

It will involve substantial investments in the early years for the construction and operation of ship and shore facilities for research and surveys, the development of new instruments for charting the seas and gathering data, and the training of new scientific manpower.

We are just at the threshold of our knowledge of the oceans. Already their military importance, their potential use for weather predictions, for food, and for minerals are evident. Further research will undoubtedly disclose additional uses.

Knowledge of the oceans is more than a matter of curiosity. Our very survival may hinge upon it. Although understanding of our marine environment and maps of the ocean floor would afford to our military forces a demonstrable advantage, we have thus far neglected oceanography. We do not have adequate charts of more than one or two percent of the oceans.

The seas also offer a wealth of nutritional resources. They already are a principal source of protein. They can provide many times the current food supply if we but learn how to garner and husband this self renewing larder. To meet the vast needs of an expanding population, the bounty of the sea must be made more available. Within two decades, our own nation will require over a million more tons of seafood than we now harvest.

Mineral resources on land will ultimately reach their limits.

But the oceans hold untapped sources of such basic minerals as salt, potassium, and magnesium in virtually limitless quantities. We will be able to extract additional elements from sea water, such as manganese, nickel, cobalt, and other elements known to abound on the ocean floor, as soon as the processes are developed to make it economically feasible.

To predict, and perhaps some day to control, changes in weather and climate is of the utmost importance to man everywhere. These changes are controlled to a large and yet unknown extent by what happens in the ocean. Ocean and atmosphere work together in a still mysterious way to determine our climate. Additional research is necessary to identify the factors in this interplay.

These are some of the reasons which compel us to embark upon a national effort in oceanography. I am therefore requesting funds for 1962 which will nearly double our government's investment over 1961, and which will provide $23,000,000 more for oceanography than what was recommended in the 1962 budget submitted earlier . . .

Knowledge and understanding of the oceans promise to assume greater and greater importance in the future. This is not a one-year program—or even a ten-year program. It is the first step in a continuing effort to acquire and apply the information about a part of our world that will ultimately determine conditions of life in the rest of the world. The opportunities are there. A vigorous program will capture these opportunities.

Partially as a result of President Kennedy's foresight and courage, the Magnuson Bill passed the Senate late in 1962. This was designed to advance the marine sciences by establishing a comprehensive 10-year program of oceanographic research. Subsequently, man's knowledge of and exploration of the sea advanced in rapid proportions. Within a few years after the passage of the Magnuson Bill, the growing oceanographic sciences had already produced numerous tangible results of benefit to mankind. Inevitably, this will lead to underwater farming, mining, power production, ranching, and manufacturing on levels approaching those which exist on land. A new breed of underwater scientists and engineers has been an outgrowth of the increased emphasis on underwater exploration.

As great as has been the rise of interest in the sea, almost equally as great has been the tendency to expect too much from it. The so-called harvest of the sea may not prove to be as great as some experts once anticipated. In fact, many ecologists now state quite firmly that we cannot depend on the oceans as we once anticipated.

Much of the problem Americans now face regarding their water resources is attributable to pollution. Governmental and private studies in recent years have uncovered an alarming amount of water pollution due to industrial dyes, insoluble detergents, radioactive materials, and the like, all of which have turned up in alarmingly greater amounts in our rivers, lakes, and other natural water reservoirs in the past decade.

Many cities must seek new sources of water supply in distant reservoirs because their own supplies have been exhausted. Millions of dollars have been spent on long-distance pipelines, and American government officials have been looking more and more toward freshwater reservoirs in Canada. The pressures of the expanding American population have created a tremendous demand for new sources of fresh water.

Eventually, many people concerned with America's water supply feel, the government will have to sponsor the development of a network of plants for water reclamation. These plants will reclaim, re-process, and re-distribute the same water that has been polluted. Pilot plants for water reclamation began operating not too long ago in California, Illinois, Florida, and Maryland.

A beneficial by-product of water reclamation would be fertilizer. The filtered wastes will be separated into harmful and non-harmful solids. The harmful wastes can be neutralized with chemicals, and the non-harmful solids can be packaged or piped off as agricultural fertilizers.

At one time it was thought that man could bury atomic wastes in the depths of the ocean, and that they would remain there forever. But an expedition, led by the son of Auguste Picard in a bathysphere called the Trieste, proved otherwise. The young Picard and an American naval officer went down into a deep trench where they found the tide still able to penetrate. They deduced that, in time, the currents in the trench would force the very waste materials that had been presumed buried forever, back to the surface. This expedition proved the unfeasibility of burying atomic wastes in the ocean depths, and that other means must be found.

This question of buried material resurfacing after it has been dropped beneath the sea received considerable attention and publicity in the summer of 1970 when the Army dumped poison gas in concrete containers into the Atlantic Ocean. No one has ever fully explained what might happen should the concrete fail to hold up and release the poisonous gases in the lower depths of the ocean. This is the type of situation that can no longer be overlooked. We must begin to realize that even the sea has its limits.

In fact, there may be areas concerning the sea that should be left unexplored. A few years ago, a plan called the Mohole Project was formulated in which a group of leading oceanographers announced its intention of drilling through the earth crust, at a spot where the crust was thinnest at the bottom of the ocean.

Before the project was launched, Dr. Theodore O'Donnell Iselin, a noted anthropologist, was consulted. He expressed grave reservations regarding the project. He claimed it wasn't wise to attempt to drill through the earth crust because the results of such a move, uncharted as they were, could prove disastrous. He pointed out the possibilities of the water disappearing in some way, or of earthquakes being caused. Obviously, the prospect of such monumental consequences must be heavily weighed in relation to the possibility of deriving benefits from underwater experimentation.

How do you, as a new diver, fit in the ranks of modern water pioneers? A good diver is a person who can act intelligently and with control toward a certain objective. He is confident in the knowledge that he is aware of everything he may encounter underwater, and that he is prepared to cope with it. This knowledge can come only from experience, long experience, and this is not easily or carelessly acquired.

Only the limits of your appreciation and curiosity of the sea will limit how far you go as a diver. The sea's magic and mystery are open to nearly all who choose to become part of it, and this is how you can carry on your role as a pioneer, restricted only by your own will, and not by outside factors.

Above all, entrance to the sea is a privilege not to be abused. The sea will yield its mysteries and phenomena only if treated with patience and respect. You can come to terms with it, but never master it. It is marvelous enough that man has come to the point where he is privileged to wander the ocean floors.

It is a privilege that has few equals on earth. And only we divers can fully appreciate it.

DECOMPRESSION PROCEDURES

GENERAL INSTRUCTIONS FOR AIR DIVING

Need for Decompression

A quantity of nitrogen is taken up by the body during every dive. The amount absorbed depends upon the depth of the dive and the exposure (bottom) time. If the quantity of nitrogen dissolved in the body tissues exceeds a certain critical amount, the ascent must be delayed to allow the body tissue to remove the excess nitrogen. Decompression sickness results from failure to delay the ascent and to allow this process of gradual desaturation. A specified time at a specific depth for purposes of desaturation is called a decompression stop.

"No Decompression" Schedules

Dives that are not long or deep enough to require decompression stops are "no decompression" dives. Dives to 33 feet or less do not require decompression stops. As the depth increases, the allowable bottom time for "no decompression" dives decreases. Five minutes at 190 feet is the shortest and deepest "no decompression" schedule. These dives are all listed in the No Decompression Limits and Repetitive Group Designation Table for "No Decompression" Dives, ("No Decompression Table" (table 1-6)) and only require compliance with the 60 feet per minute rate of ascent.

Schedules That Require Decompression Stops

All dives beyond the limits of the "No Decompression Table" require decompression stops. These dives are listed in the Navy Standard Air Decompression Table (table 1-5). Comply exactly with instructions except as modified by surface decompression procedures.

Variations in Rate of Ascent

Ascend from all dives at the rate of 60 feet per minute.
In the event you exceed the 60 feet per minute rate:
  (1) If no decompression stops are required, but the bottom time places you within 10 minutes of a schedule that does require decompression; stop at 10 feet for the time that you should have taken in ascent at 60 feet per minute.
  (2) If decompression is required; stop 10 feet below the first listed decompression depth for the time that you should have taken in ascent at 60 feet per minute.
In the event you are unable to maintain the 60 feet per minute rate of ascent:
  (1) If the delay was within 30 feet of the bottom; add to the bottom time, the additional time used in ascent. Decompress according to the requirements of the total bottom time. This is the safer procedure.
  (2) If the delay was above 30 feet from the bottom; increase the first stop by the difference between the time consumed in ascent and the time that should have been consumed at 60 feet per minute.

Repetitive Dive Procedure

A dive performed within 12 hours of surfacing from a previous dive is a repetitive dive. The period between dives is the surface interval. Excess nitrogen requires 12 hours to effectively be lost from the body. These tables are designed to protect the diver from the effects of this residual nitrogen. Allow a minimum surface interval of 10 minutes between all dives. Specific instructions are given for the use of each table in the following order:
  (1) The "No Decompression Table" or the Navy Standard Air Decompression Table gives the repetitive group designation for all schedules which may preceed a repetitive dive.
  (2) The Surface Interval Credit Table gives credit for the desaturation occurring during the surface interval.
  (3) The Repetitive Dive Timetable gives the number of minutes or residual nitrogen time to add to the actual bottom time of the repetitive dive in order to obtain decompression for the residual nitrogen.
  (4) The "No Decompression Table" or the Navy Standard Air Decompression Table gives the decompression required for the repetitive dive.

U.S. NAVY STANDARD AIR DECOMPRESSION TABLE

INSTRUCTIONS FOR USE

Time of decompression stops in the table is in minutes.
Enter the table at the exact or the next greater depth than the maximum depth attained during the dive. Select the listed bottom time that is exactly equal to or is next greater than the bottom time of the dive. Maintain the diver's chest as close as possible to each decompression depth for the number of minutes listed. The rate of ascent between stops is not critical. Commence timing each stop on arrival at the decompression depth and resume ascent when the specified time has lapsed.
For example – a dive to 82 feet for 36 minutes. To determine the proper decompression procedure: The next greater depth listed in this table is 90 feet. The next greater bottom time listed opposite 90 feet is 40. Stop 7 minutes at 10 feet in accordance with the 90/40 schedule.
For example – a dive to 110 feet for 30 minutes. It is known that the depth did not exceed 110 feet. To determine the proper decompression schedule: The exact depth of 110 feet is listed. The exact bottom time of 30 minutes is listed opposite 110 feet. Decompress according to the 110/30 schedule unless the dive was particularly cold or arduous. In that case, go to the 110/40, the 120/30, or the 120/40 at your own discretion.   (Rev. 1958)

U.S. NAVY STANDARD AIR DECOMPRESSION TABLE

DEPTH (ft)	BOTTOM TIME (mins)	TIME TO FIRST STOP	50	40	30	20	10	TOTAL ASCENT TIME	REPET. GROUP
40	200						0	0.7	*
	210	0.5					2	2.5	N
	230	0.5					7	7.5	N
	250	0.5					11	11.5	O
	270	0.5					15	15.5	O
	300	0.5					19	19.5	Z
50	100						0	0.8	*
	110	0.7					3	3.7	L
	120	0.7					5	5.7	M
	140	0.7					10	10.7	M
	160	0.7					21	21.7	N
	180	0.7					29	29.7	O
	200	0.7					35	35.7	O
	220	0.7					40	40.7	Z
	240	0.7					47	47.7	Z
60	60						0	1.0	*
	70	0.8					2	2.8	K
	80	0.8					7	7.8	L
	100	0.8					14	14.8	M
	120	0.8					26	26.8	N
	140	0.8					39	39.8	O
	160	0.8					48	48.8	Z
	180	0.8					56	56.8	Z
	200	0.6				1	69	70.6	Z
70	50						0	1.2	*
	60	1.0					8	9.0	K
	70	1.0					14	15.0	L
	80	1.0					18	19.0	M
	90	1.0					23	24.0	N
	100	1.0					33	34.0	N
	110	0.8				2	41	43.8	O
	120	0.8				4	47	51.8	O
	130	0.8				6	52	58.8	O
	140	0.8				8	56	64.8	Z
	150	0.8				9	61	70.8	Z
	160	0.8				13	72	85.8	Z
	170	0.8				19	79	98.8	Z
80	40						0	1.3	*
	50	1.2					10	11.2	K
	60	1.2					17	18.2	L
	70	1.2					23	24.2	M
	80	1.0				2	31	34.0	N
	90	1.0				7	39	47.0	N
	100	1.0				11	46	58.0	O
	110	1.0				13	53	67.0	O
	120	1.0				17	56	74.0	Z
	130	1.0				19	63	83.0	Z
	140	1.0				26	69	96.0	Z
	150	1.0				32	77	110.0	Z
90	30						0	1.5	*
	40	1.3					7	8.3	J
	50	1.3					18	19.3	L
	60	1.3					25	26.3	M
	70	1.2				7	30	38.2	N
	80	1.2				13	40	54.2	N
	90	1.2				18	48	67.2	O
	100	1.2				21	54	76.2	Z
	110	1.2				24	61	86.2	Z
	120	1.2				32	68	101.2	Z
	130	1.0			5	36	74	116.0	Z
100	25						0	1.7	*
	30	1.5					3	4.5	I
	40	1.5					15	16.5	K
	50	1.3				2	24	27.3	L
	60	1.3				9	28	38.3	N
	70	1.3				17	39	57.3	O
	80	1.3				23	48	72.3	O
	90	1.2			3	23	57	84.2	Z
	100	1.2			7	23	66	97.2	Z
	110	1.2			10	34	72	117.2	Z
	120	1.2			12	41	78	132.2	Z
110	20						0	1.8	*
	25	1.7					3	4.7	H
	30	1.7					7	8.7	J
	40	1.5				2	21	24.5	L
	50	1.5				8	26	35.5	M
	60	1.5				18	36	55.5	N
	70	1.3			1	23	48	73.3	O
	80	1.3			7	23	57	88.3	Z
	90	1.3			12	30	64	107.3	Z
	100	1.3			15	37	72	125.3	Z
120	15						0	2.0	*
	20	1.8					2	3.8	H
	25	1.8					6	7.8	I
	30	1.8					14	15.8	J
	40	1.7				5	25	31.7	L
	50	1.7				15	31	47.7	N
	60	1.5			2	22	45	70.5	O
	70	1.5			9	23	55	88.5	O
	80	1.5			15	27	63	106.5	Z
	90	1.5			19	37	74	131.5	Z
	100	1.5			23	45	80	149.5	Z
130	10						0	2.2	*
	15	2.0					1	3.0	F
	20	2.0					4	6.0	H
	25	2.0					10	12.0	J
	30	1.8				3	18	22.8	M
	40	1.8				10	25	36.8	N
	50	1.7			3	21	37	62.7	O
	60	1.7			9	23	52	85.7	Z
	70	1.7			16	24	61	102.7	Z
	80	1.5		3	19	35	72	130.5	Z
	90	1.5		8	19	45	80	153.5	Z
140	10						0	2.3	*
	15	2.2					2	4.2	G
	20	2.2					6	8.2	I
	25	2.0				2	14	18.0	J
	30	2.0				5	21	28.0	K
	40	1.8			2	16	26	45.8	N
	50	1.8			6	24	44	75.8	O
	60	1.8			16	23	56	96.8	Z
	70	1.7		4	19	32	68	124.7	Z
	80	1.7		10	23	41	79	154.7	Z
150	5						0	2.5	C
	10	2.3					1	3.3	E
	15	2.3					3	5.3	G
	20	2.2				2	7	11.2	H
	25	2.2				4	17	23.2	K
	30	2.2				8	24	34.2	L
	40	2.0			5	19	33	59.0	N
	50	2.0			12	23	51	88.0	O
	60	1.8		3	19	26	62	111.8	Z
	70	1.8		11	19	39	75	145.8	Z
	80	1.7	1	17	19	50	84	172.7	Z
160	5						0	2.7	D
	10	2.5					1	3.5	F
	15	2.3					4	7.3	H
	20	2.3				3	11	16.3	J
	25	2.3				7	20	29.3	K
	30	2.2			2	11	25	40.2	M
	40	2.2			7	23	39	71.2	N
	50	2.0		2	16	23	55	98.0	Z
	60	2.0		9	19	33	69	132.0	Z
	70	1.8	1	17	22	44	80	165.8	Z
170	5						0	2.8	D
	10	2.7					2	4.7	F
	15	2.5				2	5	9.5	H
	20	2.5				4	15	21.5	J
	25	2.3			2	7	23	34.3	L
	30	2.3			4	13	26	45.3	M
	40	2.2		1	10	23	45	81.2	O
	50	2.2		5	18	23	61	109.2	Z
	60	2.0	2	15	22	37	74	152.0	Z
	70	2.0	8	17	19	51	86	183.0	Z
180	5						0	3.0	D
	10	2.8					3	5.8	F
	15	2.7				3	6	11.7	I
	20	2.5			1	5	17	25.5	K
	25	2.5			3	10	24	39.5	L
	30	2.5			6	17	27	52.5	N
	40	2.3		3	14	23	50	92.3	O
	50	2.2	2	9	19	30	65	127.2	Z
	60	2.2	5	16	19	44	81	167.2	Z
190	5						0	3.2	D
	10	2.8					4	6.8	G
	15	2.8				4	7	13.8	I
	20	2.7			2	6	20	30.7	K
	25	2.7			5	11	25	43.7	M
	30	2.5		1	8	19	32	62.5	N
	40	2.5		8	14	23	55	102.5	O
	50	2.3	4	13	22	33	72	146.3	Z
	60	2.3	10	17	19	50	84	182.3	Z

REPETITIVE DIVE TIMETABLE

REPET. GROUPS	REPETITIVE DIVE DEPTH (Ft.)															
	40	50	60	70	80	90	100	110	120	130	140	150	160	170	180	190
A	7	6	5	4	4	3	3	3	3	3	2	2	2	2	2	2
B	17	13	11	9	8	7	7	6	6	6	5	5	4	4	4	4
C	25	21	17	15	13	11	10	10	9	8	7	7	6	6	6	6
D	37	29	24	20	18	16	14	13	12	11	10	9	9	8	8	8
E	49	38	30	26	23	20	18	16	15	13	12	12	11	10	10	10
F	61	47	36	31	28	24	22	20	18	16	15	14	13	13	12	11
G	73	56	44	37	32	29	26	24	21	19	18	17	16	15	14	13
H	87	66	52	43	38	33	30	27	25	22	20	19	18	17	16	15
I	101	76	61	50	43	38	34	31	28	25	23	22	20	19	18	17
J	116	87	70	57	48	43	38	34	32	28	26	24	23	22	20	19
K	138	99	79	64	54	47	43	38	35	31	29	27	26	24	22	21
L	161	111	88	72	61	53	48	42	39	35	32	30	28	26	25	24
M	187	124	97	80	68	58	52	47	43	38	35	32	31	29	27	26
N	213	142	107	87	73	64	57	51	46	40	38	35	33	31	29	28
O	241	160	117	96	80	70	62	55	50	44	40	38	36	34	31	30
Z	257	169	122	100	84	73	64	57	52	46	42	40	37	35	32	31

(Rev. 1958)

INSTRUCTIONS FOR USE

The bottom times listed in this table are called "residual nitrogen times" and are the times a diver is to consider he has already spent on bottom when he starts a repetitive dive to a specific depth. They are in minutes.

Enter the table horizontally with the repetitive group designation from the Surface Interval Credit Table. The time in each vertical column is the number of minutes that would be required (at the depth listed at the head of the column) to saturate to the particular group.

For example – the final group designation from the Surface Interval Credit Table, on the basis of a previous dive and surface interval, is "H". To plan a dive to 110 feet, determine the "residual nitrogen time" for this depth required by the repetitive group designation: Enter this table along the horizontal line labeled "H". The table shows that one must start a dive to 110 feet as though he had already been on the bottom for 27 minutes. This information can then be applied to the Standard Air Decompression table or "No Decompression" Table in a number of ways:

(1) Assuming a diver is going to finish a job and take whatever decompression is required, he must add 27 minutes to his actual bottom time and be prepared to take decompression according to the 110 foot schedules for the sum or equivalent single dive time.

(2) Assuming one wishes to make a quick inspection dive for the minimum decompression, he will decompress according to the 110/30 schedule for a dive of 3 minutes or less (27 + 3 = 30). For a dive of over 3 minutes but less than 13, he will decompress according to the 110/40 schedule (27 + 13 = 40).

(3) Assuming that one does not want to exceed the 110/50 schedule and the amount of decompression it requires, he will have to start ascent before 23 minutes of actual bottom time (50 - 27 = 23).

(4) Assuming that a diver has air for approximately 45 minutes bottom time and decompression stops, the possible dives can be computed: A dive of 13 minutes will require 23 minutes of decompression (110/40 schedule), for a total submerged time of 36 minutes. A dive of 13 to 23 minutes will require 34 minutes of decompression (110/50 schedule), for a total submerged time of 47 to 57 minutes. Therefore, to be safe, the diver will have to start ascent before 13 minutes or a standby air source will have to be provided.

REPETITIVE DIVE WORKSHEET

I. PREVIOUS DIVE:

___ minutes ⎫ see table 1-5 or 1-6 for ⎫
___ feet ⎭ repetitive group designation ⎬ Group___

II. SURFACE INTERVAL:

___hours___minutes on surface ⎫ see table 1-7 ⎫
Group___ (from I.) ⎭ for new group ⎬ Group___

III. RESIDUAL NITROGEN TIME:

___ feet (depth of repetitive dive) ⎫ see table ⎫
Group___ (from II.) ⎭ 1-8 ⎬ ___minutes

IV. EQUIVALENT SINGLE DIVE TIME:

___ minutes (residual nitrogen time from III.)

(add) ___ minutes (actual bottom time of repetitive dive)

(sum) ___ minutes

V. DECOMPRESSION FOR REPETITIVE DIVE:

___ minutes (equivalent single dive ⎫ see table ⎫
time from IV.)
___ feet (depth of repetitive dive) ⎭ 1-5 or 1-6 ⎬

☐ No decompression required
or
Decompression stops:___ feet___minutes
___feet___minutes
___feet___minutes
___feet___minutes

"NO DECOMPRESSION" LIMITS AND REPETITIVE GROUP DESIGNATION TABLE

DEPTH (ft.)	NO DECOMPRESSION LIMITS (Min.)	REPETITIVE GROUPS														
		A	B	C	D	E	F	G	H	I	J	K	L	M	N	O
10	–	60	120	210	300											
15	–	35	70	110	160	225	350									
20	–	25	50	75	100	135	180	240	325							
25	–	20	35	55	75	100	125	160	195	245	315					
30	–	15	30	45	60	75	95	120	145	170	205	250	310			
35	310	5	15	25	40	50	60	80	100	120	140	160	190	220	270	310
40	200	5	15	25	30	40	50	.70	80	100	110	130	150	170	200	
50	100	–	10	15	25	30	40	50	60	70	80	90	100			
60	60	–	10	15	20	25	30	40	50	55	60					
70	50	–	5	10	15	20	30	35	40	45	50					
80	40	–	5	10	15	20	25	30	35	40						
90	30	–	5	10	12	15	20	25	30							
100	25	–	5	7	10	15	20	22	25							
110	20	–	–	5	10	13	15	20								
120	15	–	–	5	10	12	15									
130	10	–	–	5	8	10										
140	10	–	–	5	7	10										
150	5	–	–	5												
160	5	–	–	–	5											
170	5	–	–	–	5											
180	5	–	–	–	5											
190	5	–	–	–	5											

(Rev. 1958)

INSTRUCTIONS FOR USE

I. "No decompression" limits

This column shows at various depths greater than 30 feet the allowable diving times (in minutes) which permit surfacing directly at 60 ft. a minute with no decompression stops. Longer exposure times require the use of the Standard Air Decompression Table (Table 1-5).

II. Repetitive group designation table

The tabulated exposure times (or bottom times) are in minutes. The times at the various depths in each vertical column are the maximum exposures during which a diver will remain within the group listed at the head of the column.

To find the repetitive group designation at surfacing for dives involving exposures up to and including the "no decompression limits": Enter the table on the <u>exact or next greater depth</u> than that to which exposed and select the listed exposure time <u>exact or next greater</u> than the actual exposure time. The repetitive group designation is indicated by the letter at the head of the vertical column where the selected exposure time is listed. '

For example: A dive was to 32 feet for 45 minutes. Enter the table along the 35 ft. depth line since it is next greater than 32 ft. The table shows that since group "D" is left after 40 minutes exposure and group "E" after 50 minutes, group "E" (at the head of the column where the 50 min. exposure is listed) is the proper selection.

Exposure times for depths less than 40 ft. are listed only up to approximately five hours since this is considered to be beyond field requirements for this table.

SURFACE INTERVAL CREDIT TABLE

	Z	O	N	M	L	K	J	I	H	G	F	E	D	C	B	A
Z	0:10-0:22	0:34	0:48	1:02	1:18	1:36	1:55	2:17	2:42	3:10	3:45	4:29	5:27	6:56	10:05	12:00*
O		0:10-0:23	0:36	0:51	1:07	1:24	1:43	2:04	2:29	2:59	3:33	4:17	5:16	6:44	9:54	12:00*
N			0:10-0:24	0:39	0:54	1:11	1:30	1:53	2:18	2:47	3:22	4:04	5:03	6:32	9:43	12:00*
M				0:10-0:25	0:42	0:59	1:18	1:39	2:05	2:34	3:08	3:52	4:49	6:18	9:28	12:00*
L					0:10-0:26	0:45	1:04	1:25	1:49	2:19	2:53	3:36	4:35	6:02	9:12	12:00*
K						0:10-0:28	0:49	1:11	1:35	2:03	2:38	3:21	4:19	5:48	8:58	12:00*
J							0:10-0:31	0:54	1:19	1:47	2:20	3:04	4:02	5:40	8:40	12:00*
I								0:10-0:33	0:59	1:29	2:02	2:44	3:43	5:12	8:21	12:00*
H									0:10-0:36	1:06	1:41	2:23	3:20	4:49	7:59	12:00*
G										0:10-0:40	1:15	1:59	2:58	4:25	7:35	12:00*
F											0:10-0:45	1:29	2:28	3:57	7:05	12:00*
E												0:10-0:54	1:57	3:22	6:32	12:00*
D													0:10-1:09	2:38	5:48	12:00*
C														0:10-1:39	2:49	12:00*
B															0:10-2:10	12:00*
A																0:10-12:00*

REPETITIVE GROUP AT THE END OF THE SURFACE INTERVAL

REPETITIVE GROUP AT THE BEGINNING OF SURFACE INTERVAL (FROM PREVIOUS DIVE)

(Rev. 1958)

INSTRUCTIONS FOR USE

Surface interval time in the table is in hours and minutes ("7:59" means 7 hours and 59 minutes). The surface interval must be at least 10 minutes.

Find the repetitive group designation letter (from the previous dive schedule) on the diagonal slope. Enter the table horizontally to select the listed surface interval time that is exactly or next greater than the actual surface interval time. The repetitive group designation for the end of the surface interval is at the head of the vertical column where the selected surface interval time is listed. For example — a previous dive was to 110 ft. for 30 minutes. The diver remains on the surface 1 hour and 30 minutes and wishes to find the new repetitive group designation: The repetitive group from the last column of the 110/30 schedule in the Standard Air Decompression Tables is "J". Enter the surface interval credit table along the horizontal line labeled "J". The 1 hour and 47 min. listed surface interval time is next greater than the actual 1 hour and 30 minutes surface interval time. Therefore, the diver has lost sufficient inert gas to place him in group "G" (at the head of the vertical column selected).

*NOTE: Dives following surface intervals of more than 12 hours are not considered repetitive dives. Actual bottom times in the Standard Air Decompression Tables may be used in computing decompression for such dives.

Glossary

ABSORBENT—a substance capable of taking something into itself. Rebreathers contain a chemical absorbent which can remove carbon dioxide from expired breath.

ABYSMAL DEPTH—any vast depth. Before the advent of the bathyspheres and other modern depth-probers, this designation applied to depths below 300 fathoms.

AIR EMBOLISM—a condition in which gas expansion forces air from sacs in the lungs into blood vessels surrounding them. These bubbles act as dams when lodged in small vessels. Resultant lack of blood causes tissue to die.

ARTIFICIAL RESPIRATION—any means by which an alternating increase and decrease in chest volume is created by an outside source, while an open airway in mouth and nose passages is maintained.

BACKWASH—water piled on shore by breaking waves sets up an outward current. Also called undertow or runout.

BAROTRAUMA—injury due to effects of pressure.

BORE—a single high wave moving upstream at the mouth of a river, caused by incoming tide opposing river current.

BREAKERS—waves broken by shore, ledge, or bar.

BREAKWATER—a structure built to break the force of waves.

BREATHING AIR—commercially produced or machine-compressed air which is free of contaminating features that would harm a diver operating under pressure.

BUDDY BREATHING—an emergency technique of sharing by two or more divers of the same tank, to be used only when one diver's air supply is exhausted.

BUOYANCY—the upward force exerted upon an immersed or floating body by a fluid; neutral, positive, and negative. Neutral allows the diver to remain at a depth without effort. Positive will cause the diver to rise toward the surface and requires effort to remain at depth. Negative results in the diver's sinking toward the bottom and can be dangerous if not controlled.

CHANNEL—the deeper part of a river, harbor, or strait.

COASTAL CURRENTS—movements of water which generally parallel the shore line. Such currents may be caused by tide or wind.

CREST—maximum height of a wave.

CURRENT—a horizontal movement of water. Currents may be classified as tidal and non-tidal. Tidal currents are caused by forces of the sun and moon and are manifested in the general rise and fall occurring at regular intervals and accompanied by movement in bodies of water. Non-tidal currents include the permanent currents in the general circulatory systems of the sea as well as temporary currents arising from weather conditions.

CYLINDER—used in diving terminology to mean compressed breathing gas container.

DARK WATERS—when visibility is reduced to a minimum by material in suspension or lack of natural light.

DEBRIS—results of destruction or discard, wreckage, junk.

DECOMPRESSION—a release from pressure or compression.

DENSITY—the weight of anything per unit of volume.

DIAPHRAGM—a dividing membrane or thin partition. The thin muscle separating the chest cavity from the abdominal cavity. The rubber (or other material) separating the demand chamber in a regulator from the surrounding water.

DISLOCATION WAVES—inaccurately called "tidal waves." Caused by underwater landslides, earthquakes, or volcanic eruption.

EBB CURRENT—the movement of tidal current away from shore or down a tidal stream.

EBB TIDE—a tide that is flowing out or causing a lower water level.

EDDY—a circular movement of water, of comparatively limited area, formed on the side of a main current; may be created at points where the main stream passes projections or meets an opposite current.

ESTUARY—where tide meets river current. A narrow arm of the sea meeting the mouth of a river.

EXHALATION—the act of breathing out or emitting air from the lungs.

FACE PLATE—glass or plastic window, so constructed as to provide air space between eyes and water and to permit both eyes to see in the same plane. The skirt makes contour contact with the face, preserving air space. Pressure may be equalized by breathing into the mask. Full face plate covers eyes, nose, and mouth; regular covers eyes and nose only.

FINS—any device attached to the feet to increase area.

FLOTATION GEAR—any device employed to support the diver or to add additional emergency buoyancy.

FLOTSAM—wreckage of a ship or its cargo found floating on the sea.

FORCED WAVE—a wave generated and maintained by a continuous force.

FREE WAVE—a wave that continues to exist after the generating force has ceased to act.

FUNGUS—a group of simple plants that contain no chlorophyll and therefore must feed on living or dead plants or animals. The parasitic fungi are most dangerous to man.

GAUGE PRESSURE—the instrumental indication of change from normal atmospheric pressure level.

GROUND SWELL—large, usually smooth-swelling waves.

HEMORRHAGE—any discharge of blood from blood vessels.

HIGH WATER—the maximum height reached by a rising tide. The height may be due to periodic tidal forces alone or be augmented by weather conditions.

HOOKAH—a diving apparatus consisting of a demand regulator worn by the diver and hose connected to a compressed air supply at the surface. This is "free diving," limited to one area by the hose length.

INHALATION—the act of breathing in.

INLET—a narrow strip of water running inland or between two islands.

JETTY—a structure, as a pier, extending into a sea, lake, or river, to influence the current or tide in order to protect a harbor.

KELP—various large brown sea weeds.

KNOT—velocity unit of one nautical mile (6,080.20 ft.) per hour, equivalent to 1,689 ft. per sec. To convert ft. per. sec. into knots, multiply by 0.592.

LONGSHORE CURRENTS—movement of water close to and parallel to the shore line.

NARCOSIS—a state of stupor or arrested activity.

NAUSEA—any sickness of the stomach creating a desire to vomit.

NAUTICAL MILE—also known as a geographical mile, a unit of distance designed to equal approximately 1 minute of arc of latitude. According to the National Bureau of Standards its length is 6,080.20 feet. It is approximately 1.15 times as long as the statute mile of 5,280 feet.

PARTIAL PRESSURE—the effect of a gas exerting its share of the total pressure in a given volume.

PHYSICS OF DIVING—the science of matter and motion as related to man's activities underwater.

PHYSIOLOGY OF DIVING—the organic processes and phenomena dealing with life and functions of organs of human beings while in water environment.

RECOMPRESSION—returning the diver to highest pressure endured (or greater if necessary) for the purpose of minimizing and eliminating the effects of decompression sickness, air embolism. This process is accomplished in a recompression chamber rather than in return to depths.

REEF—a ridge or chain of rocks, sand, or coral occurring in or causing shallow areas.

REGULATOR—an automatic device for maintaining or adjusting the flow of air equal to the ambient pressure of the water.

RESPIRATORY MINUTE VOLUME—the amount of air inhaled and exhaled per minute to maintain proper body function. This is variable, depending on exertion and individual.

RUBBER SUIT—partial or complete covering for the diver, particularly useful for insulating and preserving body heat; classified as "wet" and "dry." Wet suits, usually made of foam neoprene, allow a thin layer of water to make contact with diver's skin. Dry suits, usually of rubber, prevent contact with water, but require additional insulation afforded by cloth underclothing.

RUPTURE—breaking apart, as an eardrum when pressure cannot be equalized.

SAFETY HITCH OR BUCKLE—a fastening device which must have the facility of being able to be released quickly and easily with one hand.

SANDBAR—a body of sand built up by action of waves or currents.

SCUBA—self-contained underwater breathing apparatus, any free diving unit containing the necessary elements to support life underwater.

SHOAL—shallow area of sea or river because of a bank or bar.

SINGLE HOSE UNIT—open-circuit scuba consisting of a single high-pressure hose with first stage pressure reduction at the yoke (tank attachment), second reduction at the mouthpiece. The exhaust also is at the mouthpiece.

SINUS SQUEEZE—damage to the tissue lining of the air sinuses in the head caused by failure of pressure in sinus to equalize with ambient pressure.

SKIN DIVING—diving without the use of scuba.

SNORKEL—a "J" shaped tube, the short end of which is held in the mouth, the long end extending above the surface, allowing a diver to breathe without lifting his nose or mouth out of the water while swimming face down on the surface.

SPEARGUN—any device which propels a spear from a gunlike frame, usually rubber, spring or gas-powered.

SPORT DIVER—one who dives with or without scuba for game, photographs, exploration, or other reasons.

SQUALL—a gust of wind generally accompanied by rain or snow, intense and short of duration.

SURF—waves breaking upon a shore.

SWELL—a large smooth wave.

TANKS—containers of compressed gases, also called cylinders.

TIDE—the periodic rise and fall of water level due to the gravitational properties of the moon and sun acting on the earth's rotating surface.

TIDE WAVE—a long-lasting wave that derives from the tide-producing force and displays itself in the rise and fall of the tide.

TOXIC—poisonous.

TROUGH—the hollow or low area between crests of waves.

UNDERTOW—a seaward current near the bottom of a sloping beach, caused by the return, induced by gravity, of the water carried up to the shore by waves or wind.

VALVE—a device which starts, stops, or regulates the flow of gas or air.

WAVE—a fluctuating movement in a body of water which results in an alternating rise and fall of the surface.

Index

Absolute pressure 58
Acoustics 63, 64
Air tank cylinder 37, 38, 39, 41
Air embolism 81, 82, 151
Air tank, 37, 38, 39, 40
Alexander the Great 8, 11
American Institute of Biological
  Science 120
Aqualung 14
Aquarium, saltwater 111-114
Arbolete speargun 95
Archimedes 62
Artificial respiration 151
Ascent, effects of 61, 73
Asphyxia 83
Assyrians 7
Atmosphere, pressure of 58
Australia, 133

Back roll-in entry 54-55
Bahamas, diving in 117, 135
Baja California 99
Barnacles 71, 117
Barracuda 120
Bathysphere 142
Beltran, Pepe 96
Bends (caisson disease) 19, 82, 83
Bezel 45
Bimini 135
Boarding ladder 55
Boat, diving 54, 55, 56
Borelli, Giovanni 9
Boyle's Law 58
Breath-holding 80, 81
Breder, Jr., Dr. C. M. 132
Browne, Jack 13
British Columbia 135
Buddy system 66, 87
Buoyancy 62

Caisson disease, see bends
California 135
Cameras, see photography
Canada 135
Cape Fear 135

Cape Hatteras 135
Cape Lookout 135
Cape May 135
Cape Romain 135
Carbon dioxide 77
Carbon dioxide poisoning 79
Carbon monoxide 57, 85
Carbon monoxide poisoning 85
Caribbean 99
Carolinas 135
Catalina 135
Charles' Law 61
Charles V, Emperor 9
Circulation blockage 75, 81
Closed-circuit scuba
Clown fish 133, 134
Coates, Christopher 134
Color absorption, underwater
  photography 106
Communications underwater 66
Compass, underwater 45, 46
Convulsions 83
Coral 71, 117
Corona del Mar 135
Cousteau, Jacques-Yves 13, 35, 137
Craig, Col. John D. 12
Craig-Nohl diving equipment 12
Cramps 84
Cyanosis 79

Dalton's Law 62
Davenport, Dr. Demorest 134
Davis, R. H. 12
Decompression, limits, procedures 82
Decompression sickness 84
Decompression tables 84
Decompression time 83
Defogging mask 48, 49
Denayrouse 10
Depth gauge 45, 46, 58
Desert states 135
Devil fish 126
"Diver Down" flag 28
Diving bells 9
Diver Rock 135

Diving physics 57
Diving techniques 47-64
Drowning, see safety
Dry suits 29

Electrolysis 111
Emphysema, mediastinal,
    subcutaneous 85
Enga, Dr. Edgar 12
Equipment, diving
  air valves 40, 46
  compass 45, 46
  depth gauge 45, 46, 58
  flashlight 46
  flippers, see fins 46
  floats 26, 46
  fins 24, 46
  gloves 32, 46
  goggles 23, 46
  guns, see spearguns
  hood 8, 31, 46
  inner tube 27
  knives 34, 46
  life vest 43, 46
  masks 46
  paddleboard 27
  prices 46
  pressure gauge 45
  snorkel 23, 46
  spearguns 46
  surfmats 27
  valves 46
  weight belt 42, 46
  wristwatch 45, 46
Eustachian tube 75
Exhaustion 67, 68
Exposure suits 29

Face-mask squeeze 76
Face plate 48
Fatigue 67
Feet-first dive 52, 54, 55
Film, underwater 108
Filter, underwater photography 108
Fins, full-foot, open-heel 24, 47
Fire coral 117
First aid, diving 71, 72

Fish 98
  bottom 98
  pelagic 94, 98, 100
  rock 98
Fishers Island 135
Fish, preservation of 111-114
Fitness, diving 15-20
Flag, diving 28, 46
Flashlight 46
Flat Head Lake, Mont. 135
Flippers 24, 47
Floats 26
Flotation equipment 26

Gagnan, Emile 13, 35
Galapagos Islands 124
Galatea Expedition 138
Gauge pressure 45
Gauge, depth, pressure 45
Georgia 135
Gloucester, Mass. 135
Gloves 32, 46
Goggles 23, 46
Gold River 135
Grand Isle 135
Great Barrier Reef 117
Great Lakes 135
Gulf of Mexico 135
Gulf States 135
Gulf Stream 135
Guns, underwater 46

Hackinger, Dr. Adelbert 134
Halley, Edmund 9, 10
Hand-held speargun 95
Hand signals 66, 87
"Harbormaster" 120
"Hard-hat" equipment 10, 12
Hawaiian sling speargun 95
Hazards, diving 65-87
Head-first dive 53
Health for diving 15-19
Heart massage 69, 70
Henry's Law 61
History of diving 7-13
Hood Canal 135
Hood diving 8, 31, 46

Hookah diving equipment 154
Hydrometer 111, 112
Hyperventilation 79, 80, 100

Infections 17, 71, 72, 75
Inner tube 27
International Geophysical Year 138
Inter-Governmental Oceanographic
    Commission 138
Iselin, Dr. Theodore O'Donnel 142
Isle of Shoals 135

Jellyfish 124

Kelp 127
Kennedy, President John F. 138, 140
Key Largo 135
Key West, Fla. 131, 135
Kick, dolphin 52
Kick, flutter 53
Kicking 52
Killer whale 125
Kleingert, first diving suit 10

La Jolla, Calif. 135
Lake Champlain 135
Lake Erie 135
Lake George 135
Lake Mead 135
Le Prieur, Commander 12
Life vest 43, 46
Light absorption, see underwater
    photography
Light penetration 63
Light refraction, see underwater
    photography
Line pull signals 87
Lion fish 121, 122
Long Beach, Calif. 135
Long Branch, N.J. 135
Long Island, diving on 132, 134
Lung, diving 54-64
Lung squeeze, see thoracic squeeze 73
Lusitania 12

Magnuson Bill 140
Mahole Project 142
Manta ray 126

Mask, diving 22
Moray eel 121
Middle ear 75, 76
Middle-ear squeeze 75
Montana 135
Montauk Point 132
Monterey, Calif. 135
Mouth-to-mouth resuscitation 68-70
Mullets 131
Museum of Natural History 133
Mustard coral 117

Neoprene 22, 31, 32
New England 135
New Jersey 135
New York 134
Newport 135
New York Aquarium 134
Nitrogen 82, 83
Nitrogen narcosis ("Rapture of the
    deep") 77, 78
Nohl, Max Gene 12
Nosebleed 76
Nova Scotia 135

Octopus 122
Open-circuit scuba 35
Open-heel fins 25, 131
Open-water fish, see fish, pelagic
Overexpansion of the lungs 81
Oxygen 57
Oxygen poisoning 78

Panic 68, 70
Pelagic fish 98
Phipps, Capt. William 9, 10
Photography, underwater 103-109
    cameras
    filters
    flash attachments
    light and color absorption
    light refraction
Physical condition 15
Physical fitness, see fitness, diving 15
Physiological effects of ascent 73
Physiological effects of descent 73
Picard, Auguste 142
Pliny the Elder 9

Pneumatic speargun 94, 95
Pneumothorax 85
Pollution 141
Porpoises 125
Porpoise kick, *see* kick, dolphin
Portuguese man-of-war 124, 125
Pressure gauge 45
Prying tools 32

Quebec 135

"Rapture of the deep," *see* nitrogen
    narcosis 77
Recompression 83
Recompression chamber 83
Regulator 35, 36, 37
Richelieu River 135
Rock fish 98
Rogue shark 120
Rouquayrol 10
Rubber-powered speargun 95

Safety, diving 65-92
Salvage 9, 12
San Juan Islands 135
Savannah, Ga. 135
Scissor kick, *see* kick, flutter
Scuba diving
    breath-holding 10
    depth, see charts 92-93
    skills 94, 103, 113
Sea anemone 133, 134
Sea lions 123
Sea of Cortez 135
Sea urchin 116
Seaweed, *see* kelp 27
Sharks 118-120
Shellfish 71
Shock 86
Side roll-in-entry 55
Siebe, Augustus 10
Sinuses 74, 75
Sinus squeeze 74
Skin diving
    equipment 21-34, 42, 43, 44, 45, 46
    pressure, effects of 20
    skills 94, 103, 113
Slurp gun 112

Spearfishing 93, 98, 99, 100, 101
Spearguns
    arbolete 95
    hand-held 95
    Hawaiian sling 95
    pneumatic 94, 96, 97
    spring-loaded 95
Spearheads 94, 95, 97
Spears 94, 95
Sponge divers 7
Spring-loaded speargun 95
Sting ray 116
Stonefish 122
Suits, dry, wet 29, 30, 31, 32
Suit-squeeze 31
Surfmats 27
Symbiosis 134

Tahiti, diving in 133
Tank, air, *see* air cylinder
Tanks, fish 111-114
Teeth, effects on 77
Temperature of water 67
Thoracic squeeze 73
Treasure hunting 135
Treasure map
Trieste Expedition 142
Tritonia Corporation 12

UNESCO 137
Unit failure 70
Underwater photography, see photog-
    raphy, underwater 103-109
Underwater wristwatch 45, 46

Valves
    constant-reserve J 40, 41
    straight K 40-41
Virginia 135
Vision, effects on 63

Water reclamation 141
Washington State 135
Weights-water 58
Wet suits 29

Y.M.C.A. 19